TO

_____

FROM

_____

DATE

_____

D1219362

© 2013 by Barbour Publishing, Inc.

Compiled by Snapdragon Group℠ Tulsa, OK.

ISBN 978-1-62029-194-8

All rights reserved. No part of this publication may be reproduced or transmitted for commercial purposes, except for brief quotations in printed reviews, without written permission of the publisher.

Unless otherwise noted, scripture quotations are taken from the 1582–1610 version of the Latin Vulgate known as the Douay-Rheims version with 1752 revisions by Richard Challoner. Public domain.

Scripture texts marked NABRE are taken from the *New American Bible, revised edition* © 2010, 1991, 1986, 1970 Confraternity of Christian Doctrine, Washington, D.C. and are used by permission of the copyright owner. All Rights Reserved.

Scripture texts marked RSV-CE are taken from the *Revised Standard Version of the Bible—Second Catholic Edition* (Ignatius Edition). Copyright © 2006 National Council of the Churches of Christ in the United States of America. Used by permission. All rights reserved.

Scripture texts marked NJB are taken from the New Jerusalem Bible. Copyright © 1985 by Darton, Longman & Todd and Les Editions du Cerf. All rights reserved.

Definitions were taken from *Smith's Bible Dictionary*, *Unger's Bible Dictionary*, and *Webster's New Explorer College Dictionary*.

Published by Barbour Publishing, Inc., P.O. Box 719, Uhrichsville, Ohio 44683, www.barbourbooks.com

Our mission is to publish and distribute inspirational products offering exceptional value and biblical encouragement to the masses.

Member of the
Evangelical Christian
Publishers Association

Printed in the United States of America.

THE
BIBLE
PROMISE
BOOK

Catholic Edition

BARBOUR
PUBLISHING

Contents

Introduction 6

Adversity 8

Angels 10

Anger................ 12

Anxiety 14

Attitude.............. 16

Belief................ 18

Bereavement 20

Blessings 22

Blood of Jesus 24

Challenges........... 26

Character............ 28

Charity 30

Choices 32

Comfort.............. 34

Confession........... 36

Conflict 38

Conscience 40

Contrition 42

Courage.............. 44

Covenant............. 46

Daily Walk 48

Death................ 50

Desires............... 52

Discernment 54

Discipline 56

Encouragement 58

Endurance............ 60

Enemies.............. 62

Eternal Life.......... 64

Faith 66

Faithfulness 68

Family 70

Fear 72

Forgiveness 74

Freedom.............. 76

Friendship 78

Fruit of the Spirit 80

Generosity........... 82

Gentleness........... 84

God's Will........... 86

Goodness............. 88

Grace................ 90

Guidance 92

Guilt 94

Health & Healing 96

Heaven 98

Holiness............. 100

Holy Spirit 102

Hope 104

Humility 106

Instruction.......... 108

Jesus Christ 110

Joy 112

Kindness 114

Knowledge........... 116

Life 118

Loneliness 120

Love 122

Marriage 124

Meditation.......... 126

Mercy 128

Miracles............ 130

Obedience 132

Patience	134	Trials	204
Peace	136	Trust	206
Persecution	138	Truth	208
Prayer	140	Understanding	210
Protection	142	Unity	212
Provision	144	Victory	214
Purity	146	Waiting	216
Purpose	148	Wisdom	218
Quietness & Solitude	150	Words	220
Reconciliation	152	Work	222
Redemption	154		
Relationships	156		
Repentance	158		
Respect	160		
Rest	162		
Restoration	164		
Reverence	166		
Reward	168		
Riches & Possessions	170		
Righteousness	172		
Sacrifice	174		
Salvation	176		
Scripture	178		
Seeking God	180		
Self-Control	182		
Servanthood	184		
Sin	186		
Spiritual Thirst	188		
Stewardship & Tithes	190		
Strength	192		
Suffering	194		
Talents, Gifts & Skills	196		
Temptation	198		
Thankfulness	200		
Thoughts	202		

Introduction

Let the word of Christ dwell in you richly,
teach and admonish one another in all wisdom.
Colossians 3:16 rsv-ce

The great and wonderful promises of God! They stand in our present day just as they have stood from the beginning of time, to the end of time, and forward even throughout the endless expanse of eternity. They are as certain as God Himself, as true and faithful as He is and *always* will be.

God's promises fill every book of the Bible—from the first to the last, surrounding and bringing context to every theme. If asked, many might say that the Bible is about war and death, sin and judgment, or even the timeless conflict between good and evil. Certainly there are books of history, followed by some of the most remarkable poetry ever written. The Bible holds wisdom in abundance. The Good Book, as many refer to it, also reads like a political primer. Kingdoms rising and falling. Power struggles, complex cultural conflicts, and the loyalty and heartache of family ties. It's all there in the pages of the Bible. . .laced with God's assurances, His loving words, and graceful intentions extended to whoever reaches out for them.

It could be that you are struggling today. Maybe you wonder if God cares about you and the minutia of your everyday life. You might wonder if He knows you are anxious and hurting, feeling alone and unloved, or burdened by financial or health issues. Perhaps your relationships are falling apart. Whatever it is, God wants you to know that He cares. He loves you as only a Creator can love His own creation. He longs for you to be all He has called you to be. He longs to hold you and comfort you in the palm of His mighty hand.

The book you are holding is more than a random list of scripture selections. This Bible promise book has been designed to be a source of hope—compiled especially for the Catholic reader, with the counsel and assistance of a number of believers who espouse the Catholic faith. Of course, this book is not extensive enough to cover all of life's concerns, but within its pages there are many topics that you may be wondering about. We've listed them in alphabetical order so you can easily find what you need. We have drawn these promises from many versions and parts of the Bible, and yet, they are in no way comprehensive. One source says there are 1,260 promises contained in the Bible. Another says 3,575. A third says 5,000. Even these may not represent a definitive count—especially when considering that some scriptures aren't presented in the form of a promise, but in context are filled with great hope and promise. These scriptures lift the text from ordinary to extraordinary, from enough to abundant beyond imagination. They establish the goodness and faithfulness of our God.

It is our hope that as you read through the pages of this book, your heart will be encouraged and your mind enriched. We pray that your life will be changed and your worldview enhanced. Most of all, we pray that you would see your heavenly Father in a new light—the light of His great love for you!

Adversity

*n.: A condition or experience of serious
or continued misfortune.*

When thou shalt pass through the waters, I will be with thee,
and the rivers shall not cover thee: when thou shalt walk in
the fire, thou shalt not be burnt, and the flames shall not burn
in thee: for I am the Lord thy God, the Holy One of Israel,
thy Saviour.

ISAIAS 43:2–3

The Lord is become a refuge for the poor: a helper in due time
in tribulation. And let them trust in thee who know thy name:
for thou hast not forsaken them that seek thee, O Lord.

PSALM 9:9–10

Our God is our refuge and strength: a helper in troubles, which
have found us exceedingly. Therefore we will not fear, when the
earth shall be troubled; and the mountains shall be removed
into the heart of the sea. Their waters roared and were troubled:
the mountains were troubled with his strength. The stream of
the river maketh the city of God joyful: the most High hath
sanctified his own tabernacle. God is in the midst thereof, it
shall not be moved: God will help it in the morning early.

PSALM 46:1–3

Though the Lord may give you the bread of adversity and
the water of affliction, yet your Teacher will not hide himself
any more, but your eyes shall see your Teacher.

ISAIAH 30:20 RSV-CE

Those who love me, I will deliver; I will protect those who know
my name. When they call to me, I will answer them; I will be
with them in trouble, I will rescue them and honor them. With
long life I will satisfy them, and show them my salvation.

PSALM 91:14–16 RSV-CE

The eyes of Yahweh are on the upright, his ear turned to their cry. But Yahweh's face is set against those who do evil, to cut off the memory of them from the earth. They cry in anguish and Yahweh hears, and rescues them from all their troubles. Yahweh is near to the broken-hearted, he helps those whose spirit is crushed. Though hardships without number beset the upright, Yahweh brings rescue from them all. . . . Yahweh takes care of all their bones, not one of them will be broken. Yahweh ransoms the lives of those who serve him, and there will be no penalty for those who take refuge in him.

PSALM 34:15, 17, 19–20, 22 NJB

The LORD supports all who are falling and raises up all who are bowed down. The eyes of all look hopefully to you; you give them their food in due season. You open wide your hand and satisfy the desire of every living thing. The LORD is just in all his ways, merciful in all his works. The LORD is near to all who call upon him, to all who call upon him in truth. He fulfills the desire of those who fear him; he hears their cry and saves them. The LORD watches over all who love him, but all the wicked he destroys. My mouth will speak the praises of the LORD; all flesh will bless his holy name forever and ever.

PSALM 145:14–21 NABRE

The LORD is good to those who wait for him, a refuge on the day of distress, taking care of those who look to him for protection, when the flood rages; he makes an end of his opponents, and pursues his enemies into darkness.

NAHUM 1:7–8 NABRE

Angels

*n.: In its most common use in Scripture,
the word designates certain spiritual and
superhuman beings, who are introduced
to us as messengers of God.*

To which of the angels did God ever say: "You are my son; this day I have begotten you"? Or again: "I will be a father to him, and he shall be a son to me"? And again, when he leads the first-born into the world, he says: "Let all the angels of God worship him." Of the angels he says: "He makes his angels winds and his ministers a fiery flame"; but of the Son: "Your throne, O God, stands forever and ever; and a righteous scepter is the scepter of your kingdom. You loved justice and hated wickedness; therefore God, your God, anointed you with the oil of gladness above your companions"; and: "At the beginning, O Lord, you established the earth, and the heavens are the works of your hands. They will perish, but you remain; and they will all grow old like a garment. You will roll them up like a cloak, and like a garment they will be changed. But you are the same, and your years will have no end." But to which of the angels has he ever said: "Sit at my right hand until I make your enemies your footstool"? Are they not all ministering spirits sent to serve, for the sake of those who are to inherit salvation?

HEBREWS 1:5–14 NABRE

He will give his angels charge of you to guard you in all your ways. On their hands they will bear you up, lest you dash your foot against a stone.

PSALM 91:11–12 RSV-CE

See that you despise not one of these little ones: for I say to you, that their angels in heaven always see the face of my Father who is in heaven.

MATTHEW 18:10

The angel of Yahweh encamps around those who fear him, and rescues them. Taste and see that Yahweh is good. How blessed are those who take refuge in him. Fear Yahweh, you his holy ones; those who fear him lack for nothing.

PSALM 34:7–9 NJB

In the countryside close by there were shepherds out in the fields keeping guard over their sheep during the watches of the night. An angel of the Lord stood over them and the glory of the Lord shone round them. They were terrified, but the angel said, Do not be afraid. Look, I bring you news of great joy, a joy to be shared by the whole people. Today in the town of David a Saviour has been born to you; he is Christ the Lord. And here is a sign for you: you will find a baby wrapped in swaddling clothes and lying in a manger. And all at once with the angel there was a great throng of the hosts of heaven, praising God with the words: Glory to God in the highest heaven, and on earth peace for those he favours.

LUKE 2:8–14 NJB

After withdrawing about a stone's throw from them and kneeling, he prayed, saying, "Father, if you are willing, take this cup away from me; still, not my will but yours be done." (And to strengthen him an angel from heaven appeared to him.)

LUKE 22:41–43 NAB

Anger

n.: The emotion of instant displeasure,
indignation, arising from the feeling of injury
done or intended, or from the discovery
of offense against law.

Who is a God like thee, pardoning iniquity and passing over transgression for the remnant of his inheritance? He does not retain his anger for ever because he delights in steadfast love.

MICAH 7:18 RSV-CE

O LORD, my God, I cried out to you and you healed me. LORD, you brought me up from Sheol; you kept me from going down to the pit. Sing praise to the LORD, you faithful; give thanks to God's holy name. For divine anger lasts but a moment; divine favor lasts a lifetime. At dusk weeping comes for the night; but at dawn there is rejoicing.

PSALM 30:3–6 NABRE

Put off, according to former conversation, the old man, who is corrupted according to the desire of error. And be renewed in spirit of your mind: And put on the new man, who according to God is created in justice and holiness of truth. Wherefore, putting away lying, speak ye the truth, every man with his neighbour. For we are members one of another. Be angry: and sin not. Let not the sun go down upon your anger. Give not place to the devil.

EPHESIANS 4:22–27

Grieve not the holy Spirit of God: whereby you are sealed unto the day of redemption. Let all bitterness and anger and indignation and clamour and blasphemy be put away from you, with all malice. And be ye kind one to another: merciful, forgiving one another, even as God hath forgiven you in Christ.

EPHESIANS 4:31–32

Beloved, never avenge yourselves, but leave it to the wrath of God; for it is written, "Vengeance is mine, I will repay, says the Lord." No, "if your enemy is hungry, feed him; if he is thirsty, give him drink; for by so doing you will heap burning coals upon his head." Do not be overcome by evil, but overcome evil with good.

ROMANS 12:19–21 RSV-CE

A mild answer turns away wrath, sharp words stir up anger. The tongue of the wise makes knowledge welcome, the mouth of a fool spews folly.

PROVERBS 15:1–2 NJB

This was the witness given at the appointed time, of which I was appointed herald and apostle and—I am telling the truth and no lie—a teacher of the gentiles in faith and truth. In every place, then, I want the men to lift their hands up reverently in prayer, with no anger or argument.

1 TIMOTHY 2:7–8 NJB

Trust in the LORD and do good that you may dwell in the land and live secure. Find your delight in the LORD who will give you your heart's desire. Commit your way to the LORD; trust that God will act and make your integrity shine like the dawn, your vindication like noonday. Be still before the LORD; wait for God. Do not be provoked by the prosperous, nor by malicious schemers. Give up your anger, abandon your wrath; do not be provoked; it brings only harm. Those who do evil will be cut off, but those who wait for the LORD will possess the land. Wait a little, and the wicked will be no more; look for them and they will not be there.

PSALM 37:2–10 NABRE

Anxiety

n.: A painful or fearful uneasiness of mind,
usually over an impending or anticipated event.

Blessed be the man that trusteth in the Lord, and the Lord shall be his confidence. And he shall be as a tree that is planted by the waters, that spreadeth out its roots towards moisture: and it shall not fear when the heat cometh. And the leaf thereof shall be green, and in the time of drought it shall not be solicitous, neither shall it cease at any time to bring forth fruit.

JEREMIAS 17:7–8

The Lord is my shepherd, I shall not want; he makes me lie down in green pastures. He leads me beside still waters; he restores my soul. He leads me in paths of righteousness for his name's sake. Even though I walk through the valley of the shadow of death, I fear no evil; for thou art with me; thy rod and thy staff, they comfort me. Thou preparest a table before me in the presence of my enemies; thou anointest my head with oil, my cup overflows. Surely goodness and mercy shall follow me all the days of my life; and I shall dwell in the house of the Lord for ever.

PSALM 23:1–6 RSV-CE

Be nothing solicitous: but in every thing, by prayer and supplication, with thanksgiving, let your petitions be made known to God. And the peace of God, which surpasseth all understanding, keep your hearts and minds in Christ Jesus.

PHILIPPIANS 4:6–7

There is nothing upon earth that I desire besides thee. My flesh and my heart may fail, but God is the strength of my heart and my portion for ever.

PSALM 73:25–26 RSV-CE

Anxiety in a man's heart depresses it, but a kindly word makes it glad.

PROVERBS 12:25 NABRE

If Yahweh did not come to my help, I should soon find myself dwelling in the silence. I need only say, "I am slipping," for your faithful love, Yahweh, to support me; however great the anxiety of my heart, your consolations soothe me.

PSALM 94:17–19 NJB

Jerusalem! The mountains encircle her: so Yahweh encircles his people, henceforth and for ever. The sceptre of the wicked will not come to rest over the heritage of the upright; or the upright might set their own hands to evil. Do good, Yahweh, to those who are good, to the sincere at heart.

PSALM 125:2–4 NJB

Be you humbled therefore under the mighty hand of God, that he may exalt you in the time of visitation: Casting all your care upon him, for he hath care of you. Be sober and watch: because your adversary the devil, as a roaring lion, goeth about seeking whom he may devour. Whom resist ye, strong in faith: knowing that the same affliction befalls your brethren who are in the world. But the God of all grace, who hath called us into his eternal glory in Christ Jesus, after you have suffered a little, will himself perfect you, and confirm you, and establish you.

1 PETER 5:6–10

The prayer of the poor man, when he was anxious, and poured out his supplication before the Lord. Hear, O Lord, my prayer: and let my cry come to thee.

PSALM 101:1–3

God, examine me and know my heart, test me and know my concerns.

PSALM 139:23 NJB

Attitude

n.: A way of thinking or
feeling about a fact or circumstance.

You were to put aside your old self, which belongs to your
old way of life and is corrupted by following illusory desires.
Your mind was to be renewed in spirit so that you could put
on the New Man that has been created on God's principles,
in the uprightness and holiness of the truth.

EPHESIANS 4:22–24 NJB

Do not be conformed to this world but be transformed by
the renewal of your mind, that you may prove what is the
will of God, what is good and acceptable and perfect. For
by the grace given to me I bid every one among you not to
think of himself more highly than he ought to think, but to
think with sober judgment, each according to the measure of
faith which God has assigned him.

ROMANS 12:2–3 RSV-CE

Let this mind be in you, which was also in Christ Jesus:
Who being in the form of God, thought it not robbery to
be equal with God: But emptied himself, taking the form of
a servant, being made in the likeness of men, and in habit
found as a man. Emptied himself. . .made himself as of no
account. He humbled himself, becoming obedient unto
death, even to the death of the cross.

PHILIPPIANS 2:5–8

Christ therefore having suffered in the flesh, be you also
armed with the same thought: for he that hath suffered in
the flesh hath ceased from sins: That now he may live the
rest of his time in the flesh, not after the desires of men but
according to the will of God.

I PETER 4:1–2

At this time the disciples came to Jesus and said, "Who is the greatest in the kingdom of Heaven?" So he called a little child to him whom he set among them. Then he said, "In truth I tell you, unless you change and become like little children you will never enter the kingdom of Heaven. And so, the one who makes himself as little as this little child is the greatest in the kingdom of Heaven."

MATTHEW 18:1–4 NJB

Jesus summoned them and said to them, "You know that those who are recognized as rulers over the Gentiles lord it over them, and their great ones make their authority over them felt. But it shall not be so among you. Rather, whoever wishes to be great among you will be your servant; whoever wishes to be first among you will be the slave of all. For the Son of Man did not come to be served but to serve and to give his life as a ransom for many."

MARK 10:42–45 NABRE

The love of money is the root of all evils; it is through this craving that some have wandered away from the faith and pierced their hearts with many pangs. But as for you, man of God, shun all this; aim at righteousness, godliness, faith, love, steadfastness, gentleness.

1 TIMOTHY 6:10–11 RSV-CE

With all watchfulness keep thy heart, because life issueth out from it. Remove from thee a froward mouth, and let detracting lips be far from thee. Let thy eyes look straight on, and let thy eyelids go before thy steps. Make straight the path for thy feet, and all thy ways shall be established.

PROVERBS 4:23–26

Belief

n.: Mental acceptance of
something as real or true.

He that cometh to God must believe that he is: and is a rewarder to them that seek him.

HEBREWS 11:6

Thomas, called Didymus, one of the Twelve, was not with them when Jesus came. So the other disciples said to him, "We have seen the Lord." But he said to them, "Unless I see the mark of the nails in his hands and put my finger into the nailmarks and put my hand into his side, I will not believe." Now a week later his disciples were again inside and Thomas was with them. Jesus came, although the doors were locked, and stood in their midst and said, "Peace be with you." Then he said to Thomas, "Put your finger here and see my hands, and bring your hand and put it into my side, and do not be unbelieving, but believe." Thomas answered and said to him, "My Lord and my God!" Jesus said to him, "Have you come to believe because you have seen me? Blessed are those who have not seen and have believed."

JOHN 20:24–29 NJB

God so loved the world, as to give his only begotten Son: that whosoever believeth in him may not perish, but may have life everlasting. For God sent not his Son into the world, to judge the world: but that the world may be saved by him.

JOHN 3:16–17

If I do not the works of my Father, believe me not. But if I do, though you will not believe me, believe the works: that you may know and believe that the Father is in me and I in the Father.

JOHN 10:37–38

I am come, a light into the world, that whosoever believeth in me may not remain in darkness.

JOHN 12:46

If we accept the testimony of human witnesses, God's testimony is greater, for this is God's testimony which he gave about his Son. Whoever believes in the Son of God has this testimony within him, and whoever does not believe is making God a liar, because he has not believed the testimony God has given about his Son. This is the testimony: God has given us eternal life, and this life is in his Son.

1 JOHN 5:9–11 NJB

They brought the boy to him [Jesus]; and when the spirit saw him, immediately it convulsed the boy, and he fell on the ground and rolled about, foaming at the mouth. And Jesus asked his father, "How long has he had this?" And he said, "From childhood. And it has often cast him into the fire and into the water, to destroy him; but if you can do anything, have pity on us and help us." And Jesus said to him, "If you can! All things are possible to him who believes." Immediately the father of the child cried out and said, "I believe; help my unbelief!" And when Jesus saw that a crowd came running together, he rebuked the unclean spirit, saying to it, "You dumb and deaf spirit, I command you, come out of him, and never enter him again." And after crying out and convulsing him terribly, it came out, and the boy was like a corpse; so that most of them said, "He is dead." But Jesus took him by the hand and lifted him up, and he arose.

MARK 9:20–27 RSV-CE

Bereavement

*n.: The state or fact of being deprived
of something or someone.*

We would not have you ignorant, brethren, concerning those
who are asleep, that you may not grieve as others do who
have no hope. For since we believe that Jesus died and rose
again, even so, through Jesus, God will bring with him those
who have fallen asleep. For this we declare to you by the
word of the Lord, that we who are alive, who are left until
the coming of the Lord, shall not precede those who have
fallen asleep. For the Lord himself will descend from heaven
with a cry of command, with the archangel's call, and with
the sound of the trumpet of God. And the dead in Christ
will rise first; then we who are alive, who are left, shall be
caught up together with them in the clouds to meet the
Lord in the air; and so we shall always be with the Lord.

1 Thessalonians 4:13–17 rsv-ce

Then I saw a new heaven and a new earth. The former
heaven and the former earth had passed away, and the sea
was no more. I also saw the holy city, a new Jerusalem,
coming down out of heaven from God, prepared as a bride
adorned for her husband. I heard a loud voice from the
throne saying, "Behold, God's dwelling is with the human
race. He will dwell with them and they will be his people
and God himself will always be with them (as their God).
He will wipe every tear from their eyes, and there shall be
no more death or mourning, wailing or pain, (for) the old
order has passed away."

Revelation 21:1–4 nabre

Blessed are they that mourn: for they shall be comforted.

MATTHEW 5:4

I tell you this, brethren: flesh and blood cannot inherit the kingdom of God, nor does the perishable inherit the imperishable. Lo! I tell you a mystery. We shall not all sleep, but we shall all be changed, in a moment, in the twinkling of an eye, at the last trumpet. For the trumpet will sound, and the dead will be raised imperishable, and we shall be changed. For this perishable nature must put on the imperishable, and this mortal nature must put on immortality. When the perishable puts on the imperishable, and the mortal puts on immortality, then shall come to pass the saying that is written: "Death is swallowed up in victory." "O death, where is thy victory? O death, where is thy sting?" The sting of death is sin, and the power of sin is the law. But thanks be to God, who gives us the victory through our Lord Jesus Christ.

1 CORINTHIANS 15:50–57 RSV-CE

If the dead rise not again, neither is Christ risen again. And if Christ be not risen again, your faith is vain: for you are yet in your sins. Then they also that are fallen asleep in Christ are perished. If in this life only we have hope in Christ, we are of all men most miserable. But now Christ is risen from the dead, the firstfruits of them that sleep: For by a man came death: and by a man the resurrection of the dead. And as in Adam all die, so also in Christ all shall be made alive.

1 CORINTHIANS 15:16–22

Blessings

n.: The endowment of something
conducive to happiness or welfare.

If thou wilt hear the voice of all his commandments, which I command thee this day, the Lord thy God will make thee higher than all the nations that are on the earth. And all these blessings shall come upon thee and overtake thee: yet so if thou hear his precepts. Blessed shalt thou be in the city, and blessed in the field. Blessed shall be the fruit of thy womb, and the fruit of thy ground, and the fruit of thy cattle, the droves of thy herds, and the folds of thy sheep. Blessed shall be thy barns and blessed thy stores. Blessed shalt thou be coming in and going out.

DEUTERONOMY 28:1–6

The LORD will affirm his blessing upon you, on your barns and on all your undertakings, blessing you in the land that the LORD, your God, gives you. Provided that you keep the commandments of the LORD, your God, and walk in his ways, he will establish you as a people sacred to himself, as he swore to you.

DEUTERONOMY 28:8–9 NABRE

Bring the full tithes into the storehouse, that there may be food in my house; and thereby put me to the test, says the LORD of hosts, if I will not open the windows of heaven for you and pour down for you an overflowing blessing. I will rebuke the devourer for you, so that it will not destroy the fruits of your soil; and your vine in the field shall not fail to bear, says the LORD of hosts. Then all nations will call you blessed, for you will be a land of delight, says the LORD of hosts.

MALACHI 3:10–12 RSV-CV

Opening his mouth he taught them, saying: Blessed are the poor in spirit: for theirs is the kingdom of heaven. Blessed are the meek: for they shall possess the land. Blessed are they that mourn: for they shall be comforted. Blessed are they that hunger and thirst after justice: for they shall have their fill. Blessed are the merciful: for they shall obtain mercy. Blessed are the clean of heart: they shall see God. Blessed are the peacemakers: for they shall be called the children of God.

MATTHEW 5:3–9

Blessed be God the Father of our Lord Jesus Christ, who has blessed us with all the spiritual blessings of heaven in Christ. Thus he chose us in Christ before the world was made to be holy and faultless before him in love, marking us out for himself beforehand, to be adopted sons, through Jesus Christ. Such was his purpose and good pleasure, to the praise of the glory of his grace, his free gift to us in the Beloved.

EPHESIANS 1:3–6 NJB

Blessed is the man who walks not in the counsel of the wicked, nor stands in the way of sinners, nor sits in the seat of scoffers; but his delight is in the law of the LORD, and on his law he meditates day and night. He is like a tree planted by streams of water, that yields its fruit in its season, and its leaf does not wither. In all that he does, he prospers.

PSALM 1:1–3 RSV-CE

I will send down the rain in its season, there shall be showers of blessing.

EZEKIEL 34:26

Blood of Jesus

n.: The pure, sacrificial blood shed by Jesus,
God's only begotten Son, on the cross
for the sins of mankind.

Their sins and iniquities I will remember no more. Now, where there is a remission of these, there is no more an oblation for sin. Having therefore, brethren, a confidence in the entering into the holies by the blood of Christ.

HEBREWS 10:17–19

Remember that at one time you, Gentiles in the flesh, called the uncircumcision by those called the circumcision, which is done in the flesh by human hands, were at that time without Christ, alienated from the community of Israel and strangers to the covenants of promise, without hope and without God in the world. But now in Christ Jesus you who once were far off have become near by the blood of Christ.

EPHESIANS 2:11–13 NABRE

He [Jesus] took a cup, and when he had given thanks he said, "Take this, and divide it among yourselves; for I tell you that from now on I shall not drink of the fruit of the vine until the kingdom of God comes." And he took bread, and when he had given thanks he broke it and gave it to them, saying, "This is my body which is given for you. Do this in remembrance of me." And likewise the cup after supper, saying, "This cup which is poured out for you is the new covenant in my blood."

LUKE 22:17–20 RSV-CE

You were not redeemed with corruptible things, as gold or silver, from your vain conversation of the tradition of your fathers: But with the precious blood of Christ, as of a lamb unspotted and undefiled.

1 PETER 1:18–19

God proves his love for us in that while we were still sinners Christ died for us. How much more then, since we are now justified by his blood, will we be saved through him from the wrath.

Romans 5:8–9 NABRE

Christ, being come an high Priest of the good things to come, by a greater and more perfect tabernacle, not made with hand, that is, not of this creation: Neither by the blood of goats or of calves, but by his own blood, entered once into the Holies, having obtained eternal redemption. For if the blood of goats and of oxen, and the ashes of an heifer, being sprinkled, sanctify such as are defiled, to the cleansing of the flesh: How much more shall the blood of Christ, who by the Holy Ghost offered himself unspotted unto God, cleanse our conscience from dead works, to serve the living God?

Hebrews 9:11–14

Now the righteousness of God has been manifested apart from the law, though testified to by the law and the prophets, the righteousness of God through faith in Jesus Christ for all who believe. For there is no distinction; all have sinned and are deprived of the glory of God. They are justified freely by his grace through the redemption in Christ Jesus, whom God set forth as an expiation, through faith, by his blood, to prove his righteousness because of the forgiveness of sins previously committed.

Romans 3:21–25 NABRE

Challenges

*n.: A circumstance or circumstances
that must be overcome.*

The Lord God helps me; therefore I have not been
confounded; therefore I have set my face like a flint, and I
know that I shall not be put to shame; he who vindicates
me is near. Who will contend with me? Let us stand up
together. Who is my adversary? Let him come near to me.
Behold, the Lord God helps me; who will declare me guilty?
Behold, all of them will wear out like a garment; the moth
will eat them up.

ISAIAH 50:7–9 RSV-CE

Blessed be the God and Father of our Lord Jesus Christ!
By his great mercy we have been born anew to a living hope
through the resurrection of Jesus Christ from the dead,
and to an inheritance which is imperishable, undefiled, and
unfading, kept in heaven for you, who by God's power are
guarded through faith for a salvation ready to be revealed
in the last time. In this you rejoice, though now for a little
while you may have to suffer various trials, so that the genu-
ineness of your faith, more precious than gold which though
perishable is tested by fire, may redound to praise and glory
and honor at the revelation of Jesus Christ.

1 PETER 1:3–7 RSV-CE

He knoweth my way, and has tried me as gold that passeth
through the fire: My foot hath followed his steps, I have
kept his way, and have not declined from it. I have not de-
parted from the commandments of his lips, and the words
of his mouth I have hid in my bosom.

JOB 23:10–12

We also having so great a cloud of witnesses over our head, laying aside every weight and sin which surrounds us, let us run by patience to the fight proposed to us: Looking on Jesus, the author and finisher of faith, who, having joy set before him, endured the cross, despising the shame, and now sitteth on the right hand of the throne of God. For think diligently upon him that endured such opposition from sinners against himself that you be not wearied, fainting in your minds. For you have not yet resisted unto blood, striving against sin.

HEBREWS 12:1–4

Put on the full armour of God so as to be able to resist the devil's tactics. For it is not against human enemies that we have to struggle, but against the principalities and the ruling forces who are masters of the darkness in this world, the spirits of evil in the heavens. That is why you must take up all God's armour, or you will not be able to put up any resistance on the evil day, or stand your ground even though you exert yourselves to the full.

EPHESIANS 6:11–13 NJB

My child, if you aspire to serve the Lord, prepare yourself for an ordeal. Be sincere of heart, be steadfast, and do not be alarmed when disaster comes. Cling to him and do not leave him, so that you may be honoured at the end of your days. Whatever happens to you, accept it, and in the uncertainties of your humble state, be patient, since gold is tested in the fire, and the chosen in the furnace of humiliation. Trust him and he will uphold you, follow a straight path and hope in him.

ECCLESIASTICUS 2:1–6 NJB

Character

n.: A state of moral excellence or strength.

Watch yourself in everything you do; this is also the way to keep the commandments.

ECCLESIASTICUS 32:23 NJB

Maintain good conduct among the Gentiles, so that in case they speak against you as wrongdoers, they may see your good deeds and glorify God on the day of visitation.

1 PETER 2:12 RSV-CE

With all watchfulness keep thy heart, because life issueth out from it. Remove from thee a froward mouth, and let detracting lips be far from thee. Let thy eyes look straight on, and let thy eyelids go before thy steps. Make straight the path for thy feet, and all thy ways shall be established. Decline not to the right hand, nor to the left: turn away thy foot from evil. For the Lord knoweth the ways that are on the right hand: but those are perverse which are on the left hand. But he will make thy courses straight, he will bring forward thy ways in peace.

PROVERBS 4:23–27

Gain the love of the community, in the presence of the great bow your head. To the poor lend an ear, and courteously return the greeting. Save the oppressed from the hand of the oppressor, and do not be mean-spirited in your judgments.

ECCLESIASTICUS 4:7–9 NJB

Do not set your heart on ill-gotten gains, they will be of no use to you on the day of disaster. Do not winnow in every wind, or walk along every by-way (as the double-talking sinner does). Be steady in your convictions, and be a person of your word. Be quick to listen, and deliberate in giving an answer.

ECCLESIASTICUS 5:8–11 NJB

O Lord, who shall sojourn in thy tent? Who shall dwell on thy holy hill? He who walks blamelessly, and does what is right, and speaks truth from his heart; who does not slander with his tongue, and does no evil to his friend, nor takes up a reproach against his neighbor; in whose eyes a reprobate is despised, but who honors those who fear the Lord; who swears to his own hurt and does not change; who does not put out his money at interest, and does not take a bribe against the innocent. He who does these things shall never be moved.

PSALM 15:1–5 RSV-CE

He that hath looked into the perfect law of liberty and hath continued therein, not becoming a forgetful hearer but a doer of the work: this man shall be blessed in his deed.

JAMES 1:25

A good name is more desirable than great riches, and high esteem, than gold and silver.

PROVERBS 22:1 NABRE

Do everything without grumbling or questioning, that you may be blameless and innocent, children of God without blemish in the midst of a crooked and perverse generation, among whom you shine like lights in the world.

PHILIPPIANS 2:14–15 NABRE

Who is a wise man and endued with knowledge, among you? Let him shew, by a good contestation, his work in the meekness of wisdom.

JAMES 3:18

Admonish them to be subject to princes and powers, to obey at a word, to be ready to every good work. To speak evil of no man, not to be litigious but gentle: shewing all mildness towards all men.

TITUS 3:1–2

Charity

n.: The giving of aid to the poor and suffering.

He [Jesus] said to him also that had invited him: When
thou makest a dinner or a supper, call not thy friends nor thy
brethren nor thy kinsmen nor thy neighbours who are rich;
lest perhaps they also invite thee again, and a recompense
be made to thee. But when thou makest a feast, call the
poor, the maimed, the lame and the blind. And thou shalt
be blessed, because they have not wherewith to make thee
recompense: for recompense shall be made thee at the resurrection of the just.

LUKE 14:12–14

I give thanks to my God, always making a remembrance
of thee in my prayers. Hearing of thy charity and faith,
which thou hast in the Lord Jesus and towards all the saints:
that the communication of thy faith may be made evident
in the acknowledgment of every good work that is in you in
Christ Jesus. For I have had great joy and consolation in thy
charity, because the bowels of the saints have been refreshed
by thee, brother.

PHILEMON 1:4–7

Defraud not the poor of alms, and turn not away thy eyes from
the poor. Despise not the hungry soul: and provoke not the
poor in his want. Afflict not the heart of the needy, and defer
not to gibe to him that is in distress. Reject not the petition of
the afflicted: and turn not away thy face from the needy.

ECCLESIASTICUS 4:1–4

When you give alms, do not let your left hand know what
your right hand is doing, so that your alms may be in secret;
and your Father who sees in secret will reward you.

MATTHEW 6:1–2 RSV-CE

As great as his mercy, so is his severity; he [God] judges each person as his deeds deserve: the sinner will not escape with his ill-gotten gains nor the patience of the devout go for nothing. He takes note of every charitable action, and everyone is treated as he deserves.

ECCLESIASTICUS 16:12–14 NJB

[Jesus said] "Beware of practicing your piety before men in order to be seen by them; for then you will have no reward from your Father who is in heaven. Thus, when you give alms, sound no trumpet before you, as the hypocrites do in the synagogues and in the streets, that they may be praised by men. Truly, I say to you, they have received their reward."

MATTHEW 6:1–2 RSV-CE

The righteous will answer him and say, "Lord, when did we see you hungry and feed you, or thirsty and give you drink? When did we see you a stranger and welcome you, or naked and clothe you? When did we see you ill or in prison, and visit you?" And the king will say to them in reply, "Amen, I say to you, whatever you did for one of these least brothers of mine, you did for me."

MATTHEW 25:37–40 NABRE

Blessed is he who considers the poor! The Lord delivers him in the day of trouble; the Lord protects him and keeps him alive; he is called blessed in the land; thou dost not give him up to the will of his enemies. The Lord sustains him on his sickbed; in his illness thou healest all his infirmities.

PSALM 41:1–3 RSV-CE

Choices

n.: A person or thing chosen.

The way of a fool is right in his own eyes, but a wise man listens to advice.

PROVERBS 12:15 RSV-CE

Consider your own calling, brothers. Not many of you were wise by human standards, not many were powerful, not many were of noble birth. Rather, God chose the foolish of the world to shame the wise, and God chose the weak of the world to shame the strong, and God chose the lowly and despised of the world, those who count for nothing, to reduce to nothing those who are something, so that no human being might boast before God. It is due to him that you are in Christ Jesus, who became for us wisdom from God, as well as righteousness, sanctification, and redemption, so that, as it is written, "Whoever boasts, should boast in the Lord."

1 CORINTHIANS 1:26–31 NABRE

"You did not choose me, but I chose you and appointed you that you should go and bear fruit and that your fruit should abide; so that whatever you ask the Father in my name, he may give it to you. This I command you, to love one another. If the world hates you, know that it has hated me before it hated you. If you were of the world, the world would love its own; but because you are not of the world, but I chose you out of the world, therefore the world hates you. Remember the word that I said to you, 'A servant is not greater than his master.' If they persecuted me, they will persecute you; if they kept my word, they will keep yours also."

JOHN 15:16–20 RSV-CE

I call heaven and earth to witness this day, that I have set before you life and death, blessing and cursing. Choose therefore life, that both thou and thy seed may live.

DEUTERONOMY 30:19

I gave you a land, in which you had not laboured, and cities to dwell in which you built not, vineyards and oliveyards, which you planted not. Now therefore fear the Lord, and serve him with a perfect and most sincere heart: and put away the gods which your fathers served in Mesopotamia and in Egypt, and serve the Lord. But if it seem evil to you to serve the Lord, you have your choice: choose this day that which pleaseth you, whom you would rather serve, whether the gods which your fathers served in Mesopotamia, or the gods of the Amorrhites, in whose land you dwell: but as for me and my house we will serve thee Lord, And the people answered, and said, God forbid we should leave the Lord, and serve strange gods.

JOSHUA 24:12–16

He [Jesus] came to a village, and a woman named Martha welcomed him into her house. She had a sister called Mary, who sat down at the Lord's feet and listened to him speaking. Now Martha, who was distracted with all the serving, came to him and said, "Lord, do you not care that my sister is leaving me to do the serving all by myself? Please tell her to help me." But the Lord answered, "Martha, Martha," he said, "you worry and fret about so many things, and yet few are needed, indeed only one. It is Mary who has chosen the better part, and it is not to be taken from her."

LUKE 10:38–42 NJB

Comfort

*n.: Acts or words that give strength
and hope while easing someone's grief or trouble.*

Christ did not please himself: but, as it is written: The re-
proaches of them that reproached thee fell upon me. For
what things soever were written were written for our learning: that, through patience and the comfort of the scriptures,
we might have hope.

ROMANS 15:3–4

Blessed be the God and Father of our Lord Jesus Christ,
the Father of mercies and the God of all comfort: Who
comforteth us in all our tribulation, that we also may be able
to comfort them who are in all distress, by the exhortation
wherewith we also are exhorted by God.

2 CORINTHIANS 1:3–4

The Lord is my shepherd, I shall not want; he makes me lie
down in green pastures. He leads me beside still waters; he
restores my soul. He leads me in paths of righteousness for
his name's sake. Even though I walk through the valley of
the shadow of death, I fear no evil; for thou art with me; thy
rod and thy staff, they comfort me. Thou preparest a table
before me in the presence of my enemies; thou anointest my
head with oil, my cup overflows. Surely goodness and mercy
shall follow me all the days of my life; and I shall dwell in
the house of the Lord for ever.

PSALM 23:1–6 RSV-CE

If the Lord had not been my help, my soul would soon have
dwelt in the land of silence. When I thought, "My foot
slips," thy steadfast love, O Lord, held me up. When the
cares of my heart are many, thy consolations cheer my soul.

PSALM 94:17–19 RSV-CE

As one whom the mother caresseth, so will I comfort you,
and you shall be comforted in Jerusalem.

Isaiah 66:13

You have done great things, God, who is like you? You have
shown me much misery and hardship, but you will give me
life again, You will raise me up again from the depths of the
earth, prolong my old age, and comfort me again.

Psalm 71:19–21 NJB

On arriving, Jesus found that Lazarus had been in the tomb
for four days already. Bethany is only about two miles from
Jerusalem, and many Jews had come to Martha and Mary to
comfort them about their brother. When Martha heard that
Jesus was coming she went to meet him. Mary remained
sitting in the house. Martha said to Jesus, "Lord, if you had
been here, my brother would not have died, but even now I
know that God will grant whatever you ask of him." Jesus
said to her, "Your brother will rise again."

John 11:17–23 NJB

This is my comfort in affliction, your promise that gives me life.

Psalm 119:50 NABRE

The young girl will then take pleasure in the dance, and
young men and old alike; I shall change their mourning into
gladness, comfort them, give them joy after their troubles.

Jeremiah 31:13 NJB

The Lord accepted Job's prayer. And the Lord restored the
fortunes of Job, when he had prayed for his friends; and the
Lord gave Job twice as much as he had before. Then came
to him all his brothers and sisters and all who had known
him before, and ate bread with him in his house; and they
showed him sympathy and comforted him.

Job 42:9–11 RSV-CE

Confession

n.: The disclosure of one's sins
in the sacrament of penance.

If we say that we have fellowship with him and walk in darkness, we lie and do not the truth. But if we walk in the light, as he also is in the light, we have fellowship one with another: And the blood of Jesus Christ his Son cleanseth us from all sin. If we say that we have no sin, we deceive ourselves and the truth is not in us. If we confess our sins, he is faithful and just, to forgive us our sins and to cleanse us from all iniquity. If we say that we have not sinned, we make him a liar: and his word is not in us.

1 JOHN 1:6–10

The prayer of faith shall save the sick man. And the Lord shall raise him up: and if he be in sins, they shall be forgiven him. Confess therefore your sins one to another: and pray one for another, that you may be saved. For the continual prayer of a just man availeth much.

JAMES 5:15–16

Because the administration of this office doth not only supply the want of the saints, but aboundeth also by many thanksgivings in the Lord. By the proof of this ministry, glorifying God for the obedience of your confession unto the gospel of Christ and for the simplicity of your communicating unto them and unto all.

2 CORINTHIANS 9:12–13

Let us hold fast the confession of our hope without wavering, for he who promised is faithful.

HEBREWS 10:23 RSV-CE

What does it say? The word is near you, on your lips and in your heart (that is, the word of faith which we preach); because, if you confess with your lips that Jesus is Lord and believe in your heart that God raised him from the dead, you will be saved. For man believes with his heart and so is justified, and he confesses with his lips and so is saved.

ROMANS 10:8–10 RSV-CE

Happy the sinner whose fault is removed, whose sin is forgiven. Happy those to whom the Lord imputes no guilt, in whose spirit is no deceit. As long as I kept silent, my bones wasted away; I groaned all the day. For day and night your hand was heavy upon me; my strength withered as in dry summer heat. Selah. Then I declared my sin to you; my guilt I did not hide. I said, "I confess my faults to the Lord," and you took away the guilt of my sin. Selah.

PSALM 32:1–5 NABRE

Many also of those who were now believers came, confessing and divulging their practices. And a number of those who practiced magic arts brought their books together and burned them in the sight of all; and they counted the value of them and found it came to fifty thousand pieces of silver. So the word of the Lord grew and prevailed mightily.

ACTS 19:18 RSV-CE

John the Baptist was in the desert, proclaiming a baptism of repentance for the forgiveness of sins. All Judaea and all the people of Jerusalem made their way to him, and as they were baptised by him in the river Jordan they confessed their sins.

MARK 1:4–5 NJB

Conflict

n.: A clashing, sharp disagreement,
or mental struggle resulting from incompatible
or opposing needs, drives, wishes, or demands.

You have heard how it was said, You will love your neighbour and hate your enemy. But I say this to you, love your enemies and pray for those who persecute you; so that you may be children of your Father in heaven, for he causes his sun to rise on the bad as well as the good, and sends down rain to fall on the upright and the wicked alike. For if you love those who love you, what reward will you get? Do not even the tax collectors do as much? And if you save your greetings for your brothers, are you doing anything exceptional? Do not even the gentiles do as much? You must therefore be perfect, just as your heavenly Father is perfect.

MATTHEW 5:43–48 NJB

"Whoever would love life and see good days must keep the tongue from evil and the lips from speaking deceit, must turn from evil and do good, seek peace and follow after it. For the eyes of the Lord are on the righteous and his ears turned to their prayer, but the face of the Lord is against evildoers."

1 PETER 3:10–12 NABRE

There are six things the Lord hates, yes, seven are an abomination to him; haughty eyes, a lying tongue, and hands that shed innocent blood; a heart that plots wicked schemes, feet that run swiftly to evil, the false witness who utters lies, and he who sows discord among brothers.

PROVERBS 6:16–19 NABRE

Hatred stirs up disputes, but love covers all offenses.

PROVERBS 10:12 NABRE

Let all bitterness and wrath and anger and clamor and slander be put away from you, with all malice, and be kind to one another, tenderhearted, forgiving one another, as God in Christ forgave you.

Ephesians 4:31–32 RSV-CE

God has so composed the body, giving the greater honor to the inferior part, that there may be no discord in the body, but that the members may have the same care for one another.

1 Corinthians 12:24–25 RSV-CE

Anyone who says "I love God" and hates his brother, is a liar, since whoever does not love the brother whom he can see cannot love God whom he has not seen. Indeed this is the commandment we have received from him, that whoever loves God, must also love his brother.

1 John 4:20–21 NJB

Contend not with an influential man, lest you fall into his power. Quarrel not with a rich man, lest he pay out the price of your downfall; For gold has dazzled many, and perverts the character of princes. Dispute not with a man of railing speech, heap no wood upon his fire. Be not too familiar with an unruly man, lest he speak ill of your forebears.

Sirach 8:1–4 NABRE

Beloved, do not look for revenge but leave room for the wrath; for it is written, "Vengeance is mine, I will repay, says the Lord." Rather, "If your enemy is hungry, feed him; if he is thirsty, give him something to drink; for by so doing you will heap burning coals upon his head." Do not be conquered by evil but conquer evil with good.

Romans 12:19–21 NABRE

Conscience

*n.: The sense or consciousness of the moral goodness
or badness of one's own conduct, intentions, or character
together with a feeling of obligation to do right or be good.*

Brethren, since we have confidence to enter the sanctuary
by the blood of Jesus, by the new and living way which he
opened for us through the curtain, that is, through his flesh,
and since we have a great priest over the house of God, let
us draw near with a true heart in full assurance of faith, with
our hearts sprinkled clean from an evil conscience and our
bodies washed with pure water.

Hebrews 10:19–22 rsv-ce

Pray for us. For we trust we have a good conscience, being
willing to behave ourselves well in all things. And I beseech
you the more to do this, that I may be restored to you the
sooner. And may the God of peace, who brought again from
the dead the great pastor of the sheep, our Lord Jesus Christ,
in the blood of the everlasting testament, fit you in all goodness, that you may do his will.

Hebrews 13:18–21

For our boast is this, the testimony of our conscience that we
have conducted ourselves in the world, and especially toward
you, with the simplicity and sincerity of God, (and) not by
human wisdom but by the grace of God. For we write you
nothing but what you can read and understand, and I hope
that you will understand completely, as you have come to
understand us partially, that we are your boast as you also are
ours, on the day of (our) Lord Jesus.

2 Corinthians 12:12–14 nabre

Charge some not to teach otherwise: Not to give heed to fables and endless genealogies, which furnish questions rather than the edification of God which is in faith. Now the end of the commandment is charity from a pure heart, and a good conscience, and an unfeigned faith.

1 TIMOTHY 1:13–15

Whereunto baptism, being of the like form, now saveth you also: not the putting away of the filth of the flesh, but, the examination of a good conscience towards God by the resurrection of Jesus Christ, who is on the right hand of God, swallowing down death that we might be made heirs of life everlasting: being gone into heaven, the angels and powers and virtues being made subject to him.

1 PETER 3:21–22

The blood of goats and bulls and the ashes of a heifer, sprinkled on those who have incurred defilement, may restore their bodily purity. How much more will the blood of Christ, who offered himself, blameless as he was, to God through the eternal Spirit, purify our conscience from dead actions so that we can worship the living God.

HEBREWS 9:13–14 NJB

It is not those who hear the law who are just in the sight of God; rather, those who observe the law will be justified. For when the Gentiles who do not have the law by nature observe the prescriptions of the law, they are a law for themselves even though they do not have the law. They show that the demands of the law are written in their hearts, while their conscience also bears witness and their conflicting thoughts accuse or even defend them on the day when, according to my gospel, God will judge people's hidden works through Christ Jesus.

ROMANS 2:13–16 NABRE

Contrition

n.: The state of feeling or showing sorrow and remorse for a wrong that one has done.

Even if I saddened you by my letter, I do not regret it; and if I did regret it (for) I see that that letter saddened you, if only for a while, I rejoice now, not because you were saddened, but because you were saddened into repentance; for you were saddened in a godly way, so that you did not suffer loss in anything because of us. For godly sorrow produces a salutary repentance without regret, but worldly sorrow produces death. For behold what earnestness this godly sorrow has produced for you, as well as readiness for a defense, and indignation, and fear, and yearning, and zeal, and punishment. In every way you have shown yourselves to be innocent in the matter.

2 CORINTHIANS 7:5–11 NABRE

Lord, open my lips, and my mouth will speak out your praise. Sacrifice gives you no pleasure, burnt offering you do not desire. Sacrifice to God is a broken spirit, a broken, contrite heart you never scorn.

PSALM 51:15–17 NJB

He who takes refuge in me shall possess the land, and shall inherit my holy mountain. And it shall be said, "Build up, build up, prepare the way, remove every obstruction from my people's way." For thus says the high and lofty One who inhabits eternity, whose name is Holy: "I dwell in the high and holy place, and also with him who is of a contrite and humble spirit, to revive the spirit of the humble, and to revive the heart of the contrite."

ISAIAH 57:13–15 RSV-CE

I have indeed heard Ephraim's grieving, "You flogged me, I took a flogging, like a young, untrained bull. Bring me back, let me come back, for you are Yahweh my God! For, since I turned away, I have repented; having understood, I beat my breast. I was deeply ashamed, I blushed, aware of the disgrace incurred when I was young."

JEREMIAH 31:18–19 NJB

This is the man to whom I will look, he that is humble and contrite in spirit, and trembles at my word.

ISAIAH 66:2 RSV-CE

O Lord, thou wilt open my lips: and my mouth shall declare thy praise. For if thou hadst desired sacrifice, I would indeed have given it: with burnt offerings thou wilt not be delighted. A sacrifice to God is an afflicted spirit: a contrite and humbled heart, O God, thou wilt not despise.

PSALM 50:17–19

Alleluia! Praise Yahweh—it is good to sing psalms to our God—how pleasant to praise him. Yahweh, Builder of Jerusalem! He gathers together the exiles of Israel, healing the broken-hearted and binding up their wounds; he counts out the number of the stars, and gives each one of them a name. Our Lord is great, all-powerful, his wisdom beyond all telling.

PSALM 147:1–5 NJB

Answer me, O Lord, for thy steadfast love is good; according to thy abundant mercy, turn to me. Hide not thy face from thy servant; for I am in distress, make haste to answer me. Draw near to me, redeem me, set me free because of my enemies! Thou knowest my reproach, and my shame and my dishonor; my foes are all known to thee.

PSALM 69:16–19

Courage

*n.: The mental or moral strength to venture,
persevere, and withstand danger, fear, or difficulty.*

Strengthen ye the feeble hands, and confirm the weak knees.
Say to the fainthearted: Take courage, and fear not: behold
your God will bring the revenge of recompense: God himself will come and will save you.

Isaiah 35:3–4

Behold I command thee, take courage, and be strong. Fear
not, and be not dismayed: because the Lord thy God is with
thee in all things whatsoever thou shalt go to.

Joshua 1:9

Teach me thy way, O Lord; and lead me on a level path
because of my enemies. Give me not up to the will of my
adversaries; for false witnesses have risen against me, and
they breathe out violence. I believe that I shall see the
goodness of the Lord in the land of the living! Wait for the
Lord; be strong, and let your heart take courage; yea, wait for
the Lord!

Psalm 27:11–14 rsv-ce

Be strong and of good courage, do not fear or be in dread of
them: for it is the LORD your God who goes with you; he
will not fail you or forsake you. It is the LORD who goes
before you; he will be with you, he will not fail you or forsake you; do not fear or be dismayed.

Deuteronomy 31:6, 8 rsv-ce

I have told you all this so that you may find peace in me. In
the world you will have hardship, but be courageous: I have
conquered the world.

John 16:33 njb

Be strong and of good courage, and do it. Fear not, be not dismayed; for the Lord God, even my God, is with you. He will not fail you or forsake you.

1 Chronicles 28:20 rsv-ce

About the fourth watch of the night, he [Jesus] cometh to them walking upon the sea, and he would have passed by them. But they seeing him walking upon the sea, thought it was an apparition, and they cried out. For they all saw him, and were troubled. And immediately he spoke with them, and said to them: Have a good heart, it is I, fear ye not. And he went up to them into the ship, and the wind ceased: and they were far more astonished within themselves.

Mark 6:48–51

Be watchful, stand firm in your faith, be courageous, be strong. Let all that you do be done in love.

1 Corinthians 16:13–14 rsv-ce

I know that this will result in deliverance for me through your prayers and support from the Spirit of Jesus Christ. My eager expectation and hope is that I shall not be put to shame in any way, but that with all boldness, now as always, Christ will be magnified in my body, whether by life or by death. For to me life is Christ, and death is gain. If I go on living in the flesh, that means fruitful labor for me. And I do not know which I shall choose. I am caught between the two. I long to depart this life and be with Christ, (for) that is far better. Yet that I remain (in) the flesh is more necessary for your benefit.

Philippians 1:19–26 nabre

Covenant

n.: A solemn and binding agreement.

He has shown his people the power of his works, in giving them the heritage of the nations. The works of his hands are faithful and just; all his precepts are trustworthy, they are established for ever and ever, to be performed with faithfulness and uprightness. He sent redemption to his people; he has commanded his covenant for ever. Holy and terrible is his name!

PSALM 111:6–9 RSV-CE

As they were eating, Jesus took bread, and when he had said the blessing he broke it and gave it to the disciples. "Take it and eat," he said, "this is my body." Then he took a cup, and when he had given thanks he handed it to them saying, "Drink from this, all of you, for this is my blood, the blood of the covenant, poured out for many for the forgiveness of sins. From now on, I tell you, I shall never again drink wine until the day I drink the new wine with you in the kingdom of my Father."

MATTHEW 26:26–29 NJB

Do not forget, then, that there was a time when you who were gentiles by physical descent, termed the uncircumcised by those who speak of themselves as the circumcised by reason of a physical operation, do not forget, I say, that you were at that time separate from Christ and excluded from membership of Israel, aliens with no part in the covenants of the Promise, limited to this world, without hope and without God. But now in Christ Jesus, you that used to be so far off have been brought close, by the blood of Christ.

EPHESIANS 2:11–13 NJB

When Christ came as high priest of the good things that have come to be, passing through the greater and more perfect tabernacle not made by hands, that is, not belonging to this creation, he entered once for all into the sanctuary, not with the blood of goats and calves but with his own blood, thus obtaining eternal redemption. For if the blood of goats and bulls and the sprinkling of a heifer's ashes can sanctify those who are defiled so that their flesh is cleansed, how much more will the blood of Christ, who through the eternal spirit offered himself unblemished to God, cleanse our consciences from dead works to worship the living God. For this reason he is mediator of a new covenant.

Hebrews 9:11–15 nabre

Such is the confidence we have through Christ in facing God; it is not that we are so competent that we can claim any credit for ourselves; all our competence comes from God. He has given us the competence to be ministers of a new covenant, a covenant which is not of written letters, but of the Spirit; for the written letters kill, but the Spirit gives life.

2 Corinthians 3:4–6 njb

Blessed be the Lord God of Israel: because he hath visited and wrought the redemption of his people. And hath raised up an horn of salvation to us, in the house of David his servant.... To perform mercy to our fathers and to remember his holy testament. The oath, which he swore to Abraham our father, that he would grant to us. That being delivered from the hand of our enemies, we may serve him without fear.

Luke 1:68–74

Daily Walk

*n.: The characteristics or attributes carried out
within the boundaries of one's everyday life.*

All things that are reproved are made manifest by the light:
for all that is made manifest is light. Wherefore he saith:
Rise, thou that sleepest, and arise from the dead: and Christ
shall enlighten thee. See therefore, brethren, how you walk
circumspectly: not as unwise, but as wise: redeeming the
time, because the days are evil. Wherefore, become not unwise: but understanding what is the will of God.

EPHESIANS 5:13–17

I beseech you therefore, brethren, by the mercy of God, that
you present your bodies a living sacrifice, holy, pleasing unto
God, your reasonable service. And be not conformed to this
world: but be reformed in the newness of your mind, that
you may prove what is the good and the acceptable and the
perfect will of God. For I say, by the grace that is given me,
to all that are among you, not to be more wise than it behoveth to be wise, but to be wise unto sobriety and according as God hath divided to every one the measure of faith.

ROMANS 12:1–3

He that keepeth his word, in him in very deed the charity of
God is perfected. And by this we know that we are in him.
He that saith he abideth in him ought himself also to walk
even as he walked.

1 JOHN 2:5–6

I, the prisoner in the Lord, urge you therefore to lead a life
worthy of the vocation to which you were called. With all
humility and gentleness, and with patience, support each
other in love.

EPHESIANS 4:1–2 NJB

Blessed is the man who hath not walked in the counsel of the ungodly, nor stood in the way of sinners, nor sat in the chair of pestilence: But his will is in the law of the Lord, and on his law he shall meditate day and night. And he shall be like a tree which is planted near the running waters, which shall bring forth its fruit, in due season. And his leaf shall not fall off: and all whatsoever he shall do shall prosper.

PSALM 1:1–3

Walk in the spirit: and you shall not fulfill the lusts of the flesh. For the flesh lusteth against the spirit: and the spirit against the flesh: For these are contrary one to another: so that you do not the things that you would. But if you are led by the spirit, you are not under the law.

GALATIANS 5:16–18

Will the Lord be pleased with thousands of rams, with ten thousands of rivers of oil? Shall I give my first-born for my transgression, the fruit of my body for the sin of my soul? He has showed you, O man, what is good; and what does the Lord require of you but to do justice, and to love kindness, and to walk humbly with your God?

MICAH 6:7–8 RSV-CE

Blessed are the people who know the festal shout, who walk, O Lord, in the light of thy countenance, who exult in thy name all the day, and extol thy righteousness. For thou art the glory of their strength; by thy favor our horn is exalted. For our shield belongs to the Lord, our king.

PSALM 89:15–18 RSV-CE

Death

n.: The state of no longer being alive;
the absence of life.

He [God] shall cast death down headlong for ever: and the Lord God shall wipe away tears from every face, and the reproach of his people he shall take away from off the whole earth: for the Lord hath spoken it.

ISAIAH 25:28

Precious in the sight of the Lord is the death of his saints. O Lord, I am thy servant, the son of thy handmaid. Thou hast loosed my bonds. I will offer to thee the sacrifice of thanksgiving and call on the name of the Lord.

PSALM 116:15–17 RSV-CE

If in this life only we have hope in Christ, we are of all men most miserable. But now Christ is risen from the dead, the firstfruits of them that sleep: For by a man came death: and by a man the resurrection of the dead. And as in Adam all die, so also in Christ all shall be made alive.

1 CORINTHIANS 15:19–22

We know, if our earthly house of this habitation be dissolved, that we have a building of God, a house not made with hands, eternal in heaven. For in this also we groan, desiring to be clothed upon with our habitation that is from heaven.

2 CORINTHIANS 5:1–2

Having always confidence, knowing that while we are in the body we are absent from the Lord. (For we walk by faith and not by sight.) But we are confident and have a good will to be absent rather from the body and to be present with the Lord. And therefore we labour, whether absent or present, to please him.

2 CORINTHIANS 5:6–9

When this mortal hath put on immortality, then shall come to pass the saying that is written: Death is swallowed up in victory. O death, where is thy victory? O death, where is thy sting?

1 CORINTHIANS 15:54–55

Therefore because the children are partakers of flesh and blood, he also himself in like manner hath been partaker of the same: that, through death, he might destroy him who had the empire of death, that is to say, the devil: And might deliver them, who through the fear of death were all their lifetime subject to servitude. For nowhere doth he take hold of the angels: but of the seed of Abraham he taketh hold.

HEBREWS 2:14–15

We will not have you ignorant brethren, concerning them that are asleep, that you be not sorrowful, even as others who have no hope. For if we believe that Jesus died and rose again: even so them who have slept through Jesus, will God bring with him. For this we say unto you in the word of the Lord, that we who are alive, who remain unto the coming of the Lord, shall not prevent them who have slept. For the Lord himself shall come down from heaven with commandment and with the voice of an archangel and with the trumpet of God: and the dead who are in Christ shall rise first. Then we who are alive, who are left, shall be taken up together with them in the clouds to meet Christ, into the air: and so shall we be always with the Lord. Wherefore, comfort ye one another with these words.

1 THESSALONIANS 4:12–17

Desires

*n.: Something or someone strongly
wished for or longed for.*

There is therefore now no condemnation for those who are in Christ Jesus. For the law of the Spirit of life in Christ Jesus has set me free from the law of sin and death. For God has done what the law, weakened by the flesh, could not do: sending his own Son in the likeness of sinful flesh and for sin, he condemned sin in the flesh, in order that the just requirement of the law might be fulfilled in us, who walk not according to the flesh but according to the Spirit. For those who live according to the flesh set their minds on the things of the flesh, but those who live according to the Spirit set their minds on the things of the Spirit.

ROMANS 8:1–5 RSV-CE

Those who are living by their natural inclinations have their minds on the things human nature desires; those who live in the Spirit have their minds on spiritual things. And human nature has nothing to look forward to but death, while the Spirit looks forward to life and peace.

ROMANS 8:5–6 NJB

Make love your aim, and earnestly desire the spiritual gifts, especially that you may prophesy. For one who speaks in a tongue speaks not to men but to God; for no one understands him, but he utters mysteries in the Spirit. On the other hand, he who prophesies speaks to men for their upbuilding and encouragement and consolation. He who speaks in a tongue edifies himself, but he who prophesies edifies the church.

1 CORINTHIANS 14:1–4 RSV-CE

Trust in the Lord and do good that you may dwell in the land and live secure. Find your delight in the Lord who will give you your heart's desire.

PSALM 37:3–5 NABRE

Walk by the Spirit, and do not gratify the desires of the flesh. For the desires of the flesh are against the Spirit, and the desires of the Spirit are against the flesh; for these are opposed to each other, to prevent you from doing what you would.

GALATIANS 5:16–17 RSV-CE

What the wicked dreads will come upon him, but the desire of the righteous will be granted.

PROVERBS 10:24 RSV-CE

The way of the righteous is level; thou dost make smooth the path of the righteous. In the path of thy judgments, O Lord, we wait for thee; thy memorial name is the desire of our soul.

ISAIAH 26:8–9 RSV-CE

I desire steadfast love and not sacrifice, the knowledge of God, rather than burnt offerings.

HOSEA 6:6 RSV-CE

All of us once lived among them in the desires of our flesh, following the wishes of the flesh and the impulses, and we were by nature children of wrath, like the rest. But God, who is rich in mercy, because of the great love he had for us, even when we were dead in our transgressions, brought us to life with Christ (by grace you have been saved), raised us up with him, and seated us with him in the heavens in Christ Jesus, that in the ages to come he might show the immeasurable riches of his grace in his kindness to us in Christ Jesus.

EPHESIANS 2:4–7 NABRE

Discernment

n.: The skill of coming to know, recognize,
or discriminate mentally.

Who can discern his errors? Clear thou me from hidden
faults. Keep back thy servant also from presumptuous
sins; let them not have dominion over me! Then I shall be
blameless, and innocent of great transgression. Let the words
of my mouth and the meditation of my heart be acceptable
in thy sight, O Lord, my rock and my redeemer.

PSALM 19:12–14 RSV-CE

We have received not the spirit of the world, but the Spirit
which is from God, that we might understand the gifts
bestowed on us by God. And we impart this in words not
taught by human wisdom but taught by the Spirit, interpret-
ing spiritual truths to those who possess the Spirit. The un-
spiritual man does not receive the gifts of the Spirit of God,
for they are folly to him, and he is not able to understand
them because they are spiritually discerned. The spiritual
man judges all things, but is himself to be judged by no one.

1 CORINTHIANS 2:12–15 RSV-CE

O Lord, thou hast searched me and known me! Thou
knowest when I sit down and when I rise up; thou discernest
my thoughts from afar. Thou searchest out my path and
my lying down, and art acquainted with all my ways. Even
before a word is on my tongue, lo, O Lord, thou knowest it
altogether.

PSALM 139:1–4 RSV-CE

Let him who is wise understand these things; let him who
is prudent know them. Straight are the paths of the Lord, in
them the just walk, but sinners stumble in them.

HOSEA 14:10 NABRE

God will testify for me how much I long for you all with the warm longing of Christ Jesus; it is my prayer that your love for one another may grow more and more with the knowledge and complete understanding that will help you to come to true discernment, so that you will be innocent and free of any trace of guilt when the Day of Christ comes, entirely filled with the fruits of uprightness through Jesus Christ, for the glory and praise of God.

Philippians 1:8–11 njb

The wisdom of a prudent man is to discern his way, but the folly of fools is deceiving.

Proverbs 14:8 rsv-ce

This is my prayer: that your love may increase ever more and more in knowledge and every kind of perception, to discern what is of value, so that you may be pure and blameless for the day of Christ, filled with the fruit of righteousness that comes through Jesus Christ for the glory and praise of God.

Philippians 1:9–11 nabre

Think it over; let there be no injustice. Think it over; I still am right. Is there insincerity on my tongue, or cannot my taste discern falsehood?

Job 6:29–30 nabre

I am a very young man, unskilled in leadership. And here is your servant, surrounded with your people whom you have chosen, a people so numerous that its number cannot be counted or reckoned. So give your servant a heart to understand how to govern your people, how to discern between good and evil.

1 Kings 3:7–9 njb

Discipline

n.: Training that corrects, molds,
or perfects mental ability or moral character.

Blessed is the man whom God correcteth: refuse not,
therefore, the chastising of the Lord. For he woundeth,
and cureth: he striketh, and his hands shall heal.

JOB 5:17–18

The ear that heareth the reproofs of life, shall abide in the
midst of the wise. He that rejecteth instruction, despiseth his
own soul: but he that yieldeth to reproof, possesseth understanding. The fear of the Lord is the lesson of wisdom: and
humility goeth before glory.

PROVERBS 15:31–33

My son, neglect not the discipline of the Lord: neither be
thou wearied whilst thou art rebuked by him. For whom
the Lord loveth he chastiseth: and he scourgeth every son
whom he receiveth. Persevere under discipline. God dealeth
with you as with his sons. For what son is there whom the
father doth not correct? But if you be without chastisement,
whereof all are made partakers, then are you bastards and
not sons. Moreover, we have had fathers of our flesh for in-
structors, and we reverenced them. Shall we not much more
obey the Father of spirits and live?

HEBREWS 12:5–9

From your youth embrace discipline; thus will you find wisdom with graying hair. As though plowing and sowing, draw
close to her; then await her bountiful crops. For in cultivating
her you will labor but little, and soon you will eat of her fruits.

SIRACH 6:18–20 NABRE

Discipline is like her name, she is not accessible to many. Listen, my son, and heed my advice; refuse not my counsel. Put your feet into her fetters, and your neck under her yoke. Stoop your shoulders and carry her and be not irked at her bonds. With all your soul draw close to her; with all your strength keep her ways. Search her out, discover her; seek her and you will find her. Then when you have her, do not let her go; Thus will you afterward find rest in her, and she will become your joy. Her fetters will be your throne of majesty; her bonds, your purple cord.

SIRACH 6:23–30 NABRE

For the moment all discipline seems painful rather than pleasant; later it yields the peaceful fruit of righteousness to those who have been trained by it. Therefore lift your drooping hands and strengthen your weak knees, and make straight paths for your feet, so that what is lame may not be put out of joint but rather be healed. Strive for peace with all men, and for the holiness without which no one will see the Lord. See to it that no one fail to obtain the grace of God; that no "root of bitterness" spring up and cause trouble, and by it the many become defiled.

HEBREWS 12:11–15 RSV-CE

If we discerned ourselves, we would not be under judgment; but since we are judged by (the) Lord, we are being disciplined so that we may not be condemned along with the world.

1 CORINTHIANS 11:31–32 NABRE

Encouragement

n.: The act of inspiring with courage,
spirit, or hope; heartening.

I shall go to the altar of God, to the God of my joy. I will rejoice and praise you on the harp, O God, my God. Why so downcast, why all these sighs? Hope in God! I will praise him still, my Saviour, my God.

PSALM 43:4–5 NJB

Your kingship is a kingship for ever, your reign lasts from age to age. Yahweh is trustworthy in all his words, and upright in all his deeds. Yahweh supports all who stumble, lifts up those who are bowed down.

PSALM 145:13–14 NJB

Having the same spirit of faith, as it is written: I believed, for which cause I have spoken; we also believe. For which cause we speak also: Knowing that he who raised up Jesus will raise us up also with Jesus and place us with you. For all things are for your sakes: that the grace, abounding through many, may abound in thanksgiving unto the glory of God. For which cause we faint not: but though our outward man is corrupted, yet the inward man is renewed day by day. For that which is at present momentary and light of our tribulation worketh for us above measure, exceedingly an eternal weight of glory.

2 CORINTHIANS 4:13–17

Take heed, brethren, lest perhaps there be in any of you an evil heart of unbelief, to depart from the living God. But exhort one another every day, whilst it is called to day, that none of you be hardened through the deceitfulness of sin. For we are made partakers of Christ: yet so, if we hold the beginning of his substance firm unto the end.

HEBREWS 3:12–14

Brethren, stand fast: and hold the traditions, which you have learned, whether by word or by our epistle. Now our Lord Jesus Christ himself, and God and our Father, who hath loved us and hath given us everlasting consolation and good hope in grace, exhort your hearts and confirm you in every good work and word.

2 Thessalonians 2:14–16

God hath not appointed us unto wrath: but unto the purchasing of salvation by our Lord Jesus Christ, Who died for us: that, whether we watch or sleep, we may live together with him. For which cause comfort one another and edify one another, as you also do.

1 Thessalonians 5:9–11

He who prophesies speaks to men for their upbuilding and encouragement and consolation. He who speaks in a tongue edifies himself, but he who prophesies edifies the church. Now I want you all to speak in tongues, but even more to prophesy. He who prophesies is greater than he who speaks in tongues, unless some one interprets, so that the church may be edified.

1 Corinthians 14:3–5 rsv-ce

May the God of steadfastness and encouragement grant you to live in such harmony with one another, in accord with Christ Jesus, that together you may with one voice glorify the God and Father of our Lord Jesus Christ. Welcome one another, therefore, as Christ has welcomed you, for the glory of God.

Romans 15:5–7 rsv-ce

They strengthened the spirits of the disciples and exhorted them to persevere in the faith, saying, "It is necessary for us to undergo many hardships to enter the kingdom of God."

Acts 14:22 nabre

Endurance

n.: The ability to withstand hardship,
misfortune, or stress; steadfastness.

Make every effort to supplement your faith with virtue, virtue
with knowledge, knowledge with self-control, self-control
with endurance, endurance with devotion, devotion with
mutual affection, mutual affection with love. If these are yours
and increase in abundance, they will keep you from being idle
or unfruitful in the knowledge of our Lord Jesus Christ.

2 PETER 1:5–8 NABRE

Take, my brethren, for example of suffering evil, of labour and
patience, the prophets who spoke in the name of the Lord.
Behold, we account them blessed who have endured. You have
heard of the patience of Job and you have seen the end of the
Lord, that the Lord is merciful and compassionate.

JAMES 5:10–11

May you be strengthened with all power, according to his
glorious might, for all endurance and patience with joy, giving thanks to the Father, who has qualified us to share in the
inheritance of the saints in light.

COLOSSIANS 1:11–12 RSV-CE

Because iniquity hath abounded, the charity of many shall
grow cold. But he that shall persevere to the end, he shall
be saved. And this gospel of the kingdom shall be preached
in the whole world, for a testimony to all nations: and then
shall the consummation come.

MATTHEW 24:12–14

Laying aside every weight and sin which surrounds us, let us run by patience to the fight proposed to us: Looking on Jesus, the author and finisher of faith, who, having joy set before him, endured the cross, despising the shame, and now sitteth on the right hand of the throne of God. For think diligently upon him that endured such opposition from sinners against himself that you be not wearied, fainting in your minds. For you have not yet resisted unto blood, striving against sin.

HEBREWS 12:1–4

As for you, man of God, shun all this; aim at righteousness, godliness, faith, love, steadfastness, gentleness. Fight the good fight of the faith; take hold of the eternal life to which you were called when you made the good confession in the presence of many witnesses.

1 TIMOTHY 6:11–12 RSV-CE

Whatever was written in former days was written for our instruction, that by steadfastness and by the encouragement of the scriptures we might have hope. May the God of steadfastness and encouragement grant you to live in such harmony with one another, in accord with Christ Jesus.

ROMANS 15:4–5 RSV-CE

Count it all joy, my brethren, when you meet various trials, for you know that the testing of your faith produces steadfastness. And let steadfastness have its full effect, that you may be perfect and complete, lacking in nothing.

JAMES 1:2–4 RSV-CE

We give thanks to God always for you all, constantly mentioning you in our prayers, remembering before our God and Father your work of faith and labor of love and steadfastness of hope in our Lord Jesus Christ.

1 THESSALONIANS 1:2–3 RSV-CE

Enemies

n.: One that is antagonistic to another.

Yahweh is my light and my salvation, whom should I fear? Yahweh is the fortress of my life, whom should I dread? When the wicked advance against me to eat me up, they, my opponents, my enemies, are the ones who stumble and fall. Though an army pitch camp against me, my heart will not fear, though war break out against me, my trust will never be shaken.

PSALM 27:1–3 NJB

The wicked lie in wait to destroy me; but I consider thy testimonies. I have seen a limit to all perfection, but thy commandment is exceedingly broad. Oh, how I love thy law! It is my meditation all the day. Thy commandment makes me wiser than my enemies, for it is ever with me.

PSALM 119:95–98 RSV-CE

You have heard that it hath been said, Thou shalt love thy neighbour, and hate thy enemy. But I say to you, Love your enemies: do good to them that hate you: and pray for them that persecute and calumniate you: That you may be the children of your Father who is in heaven, who maketh his sun to rise upon the good, and bad, and raineth upon the just and the unjust. For if you love them that love you, what reward shall you have? do not even the publicans this? And if you salute your brethren only, what do you more? do not also the heathens this?

MATTHEW 5:43–47

O my God, in thee I trust, let me not be put to shame; let not my enemies exult over me. Yea, let none that wait for thee be put to shame; let them be ashamed who are wantonly treacherous.

PSALM 25:2–3 RSV-CE

You, Lord, God of tenderness and mercy, slow to anger, rich in faithful love and loyalty, turn to me and pity me. Give to your servant your strength, to the child of your servant your saving help, give me a sign of your kindness. My enemies will see to their shame that you, Yahweh, help and console me.

PSALM 86:15–18 NJB

Though I walk in the midst of dangers, you guard my life when my enemies rage. You stretch out your hand; your right hand saves me. The Lord is with me to the end. Lord, your love endures forever. Never forsake the work of your hands!

PSALM 138:7–8 NABRE

Battle this day against your enemies, let not your heart be dismayed, be not afraid, do not give back, fear ye them not: Because the Lord your God is in the midst of you, and will fight for you against your enemies, to deliver you from danger.

DEUTERONOMY 20:3–4

By mercy and truth iniquity is redeemed; and by the fear of the Lord men depart from evil. When the ways of man shall please the Lord, he will convert even his enemies to peace.

PROVERBS 16:6–7

Yahweh is my shepherd, I lack nothing. In grassy meadows he lets me lie. By tranquil streams he leads me to restore my spirit. You prepare a table for me under the eyes of my enemies; you anoint my head with oil; my cup brims over. Kindness and faithful love pursue me every day of my life. I make my home in the house of Yahweh for all time to come.

PSALM 23:1–2, 5–6 NJB

Eternal Life

n.: Life having no beginning and no end;
lasting forever.

As Moses lifted up the serpent in the desert, so must the Son of man be lifted up: That whosoever believeth in him may not perish, but may have life everlasting. For God so loved the world, as to give his only begotten Son: that whosoever believeth in him may not perish, but may have life everlasting. For God sent not his Son into the world, to judge the world: but that the world may be saved by him.

JOHN 3:14–16

You, my beloved, building yourselves upon your most holy faith, praying in the Holy Ghost, keep yourselves in the love of God, waiting for the mercy of our Lord Jesus Christ, unto life everlasting.

JUDE 1:19–20

This is the will of the Father who sent me: that of all that he hath given me, I should lose nothing; but should raise it up again in the last day. And this is the will of my Father that sent me: that every one who seeth the Son and believeth in him may have life everlasting. And I will raise him up in the last day.

JOHN 6:39–40

My sheep hear my voice. And I know them: and they follow me. And I give them life everlasting: and they shall not perish for ever. And no man shall pluck them out of my hand. That which my Father hath given me is greater than all: and no one can snatch them out of the hand of my Father. I and the Father are one.

JOHN 10:27–30

These things Jesus spoke: and lifting up his eyes to heaven, he said: the hour is come. Glorify thy Son, that thy Son may glorify thee. As thou hast given him power over all flesh, that he may give eternal life to all whom thou hast given him. Now this is eternal life: That they may know thee, the only true God, and Jesus Christ, whom thou hast sent.

JOHN 17:1–3

Being made free from sin and become servants to God, you have your fruit unto sanctification, and the end life everlasting. For the wages of sin is death. But the grace of God, life everlasting in Christ Jesus our Lord.

ROMANS 6:21–22

We ourselves also were some time unwise, incredulous, erring, slaves to divers desires and pleasures, living in malice and envy, hateful and hating one another. But when the goodness and kindness of God our Saviour appeared: Not by the works of justice which we have done, but according to his mercy, he saved us, by the laver of regeneration and renovation of the Holy Ghost. Whom he hath poured forth upon us abundantly, through Jesus Christ our Saviour: that, being justified by his grace, we may be heirs according to hope of life everlasting.

TITUS 3:3–7

We know that we are of God, and the whole world is in the power of the evil one. And we know that the Son of God has come and has given us understanding, to know him who is true; and we are in him who is true, in his Son Jesus Christ. This is the true God and eternal life.

1 JOHN 5:19–20 RSV-CE

Faith

n.: A firm belief in something
for which there is no proof.

As therefore you have received Jesus Christ the Lord, walk ye in him: Rooted and built up in him and confirmed in the faith, as also you have learned: abounding in him in thanksgiving.

COLOSSIANS 2:6–7

I bow my knees to the Father of our Lord Jesus Christ, of whom all paternity in heaven and earth is named: That he would grant you, according to the riches of his glory, to be strengthened by his Spirit with might unto the inward man: That Christ may dwell by faith in your hearts.

EPHESIANS 3:14–17

Take unto you the armour of God, that you may be able to resist in the evil day and to stand in all things perfect. Stand therefore, having your loins girt about with truth and having on the breastplate of justice: And your feet shod with the preparation of the gospel of peace. In all things taking the shield of faith, wherewith you may be able to extinguish all the fiery darts of the most wicked one. And take unto you the helmet of salvation and the sword of the Spirit (which is the word of God).

EPHESIANS 6:13–17

Faith is the substance of things to be hoped for, the evidence of things that appear not. For by this the ancients obtained a testimony. By faith we understand that the world was framed by the word of God: that from invisible things visible things might be made. But without faith it is impossible to please God. For he that cometh to God must believe that he is: and is a rewarder to them that seek him.

HEBREWS 11:1–3, 6

Jesus answering, saith to them: Have the faith of God. Amen I say to you that whosoever shall say to this mountain, Be thou removed and be cast into the sea, and shall not stagger in his heart, but believe that whatsoever he saith shall be done; it shall be done unto him. Therefore I say unto you, all things, whatsoever you ask when ye pray, believe that you shall receive: and they shall come unto you.

MARK 11:22–24

I am not ashamed of the gospel. For it is the power of God unto salvation to every one that believeth: to the Jew first and to the Greek. For the justice of God is revealed therein, from faith unto faith, as it is written: The just man liveth by faith.

ROMANS 1:16–17

Being justified therefore by faith, let us have peace with God, through our Lord Jesus Christ: By whom also we have access through faith into this grace wherein we stand: and glory in the hope of the glory of the sons of God.

ROMANS 5:1–2

O man of God, fly these things: and pursue justice, godliness, faith, charity, patience, mildness. Fight the good fight of faith. Lay hold on eternal life, whereunto thou art called and be it confessed a good confession before many witnesses.

1 TIMOTHY 6:11–12

I say, by the grace that is given me, to all that are among you, not to be more wise than it behoveth to be wise, but to be wise unto sobriety and according as God hath divided to every one the measure of faith.

ROMANS 12:3

Faithfulness

n.: The state of being consistent in keeping
promises or fulfilling duties.

I will call this to mind, as my reason to have hope: the favors
of the Lord are not exhausted, his mercies are not spent;
they are renewed each morning, so great is his faithfulness.

LAMENTATIONS 3:21–23 NABRE

Blessed be the Lord, for he has wondrously shown his
steadfast love to me when I was beset as in a besieged city. I
had said in my alarm, "I am driven far from thy sight." But
thou didst hear my supplications, when I cried to thee for
help. Love the Lord, all you his saints! The Lord preserves
the faithful, but abundantly requites him who acts haughtily.

PSALM 31:21–23 RSV-CE

I cry to God Most High, to God who fulfils his purpose for
me. He will send from heaven and save me, he will put to
shame those who trample upon me. [Selah] God will send
forth his steadfast love and his faithfulness!

PSALM 57:2–3 RSV-CE

I will give thanks to thee, O Lord, among the peoples; I will
sing praises to thee among the nations. For thy steadfast love is
great to the heavens, thy faithfulness to the clouds. Be exalted,
O God, above the heavens! Let thy glory be over all the earth!

PSALM 57:9–11 RSV-CE

Know that the Lord is God! It is he that made us, and we are
his; we are his people, and the sheep of his pasture. Enter his
gates with thanksgiving, and his courts with praise! Give thanks
to him, bless his name! For the Lord is good; his steadfast love
endures for ever, and his faithfulness to all generations.

PSALM 100:3–5 RSV-CE

I will sing of thy steadfast love, O Lord, for ever; with my mouth I will proclaim thy faithfulness to all generations. For thy steadfast love was established for ever, thy faithfulness is firm as the heavens.

PSALM 89:1–2 RSV-CE

He who dwells in the shelter of the Most High, who abides in the shadow of the Almighty, will say to the Lord, "My refuge and my fortress; my God, in whom I trust." For he will deliver you from the snare of the fowler and from the deadly pestilence; he will cover you with his pinions, and under his wings you will find refuge; his faithfulness is a shield and buckler.

PSALM 91:1–4 RSV-CE

Let us hold fast the confession of our hope without wavering, for he who promised is faithful.

HEBREWS 10:23 RSV-CE

The fruit of the Spirit is love, joy, peace, patience, kindness, goodness, faithfulness, gentleness, self-control; against such there is no law. And those who belong to Christ Jesus have crucified the flesh with its passions and desires. If we live by the Spirit, let us also walk by the Spirit.

GALATIANS 5:22–25 RSV-CE

Holy brethren, who share in a heavenly call, consider Jesus, the apostle and high priest of our confession. He was faithful to him who appointed him, just as Moses also was faithful in God's house. Yet Jesus has been counted worthy of as much more glory than Moses as the builder of a house has more honor than the house. (For every house is built by some one, but the builder of all things is God.)

HEBREWS 3:4–6 RSV-CE

Family

n.: A group of persons of common ancestry,
usually living under one roof.

"Grasp this today and meditate on it carefully: Yahweh is the true God, in heaven above as on earth beneath, he and no other. Keep his laws and commandments as I give them to you today, so that you and your children after you may prosper and live long in the country that Yahweh your God is giving you for ever."

DEUTERONOMY 4:39–40 NJB

Peter began to say to him, "We have given up everything and followed you." Jesus said, "Amen, I say to you, there is no one who has given up house or brothers or sisters or mother or father or children or lands for my sake and for the sake of the gospel who will not receive a hundred times more now in this present age: houses and brothers and sisters and mothers and children and lands, with persecutions, and eternal life in the age to come."

MARK 10:28–30 NABRE

Who shall find a valiant woman? far, and from the uttermost coasts is the price of her. The heart of her husband trusteth in her, and he shall have no need of spoils. She will render him good, and not evil all the days of her life. She hath opened her mouth to wisdom, and the law of clemency is on her tongue. She hath looked well on the paths of her house, and hath not eaten her bread idle. Her children rose up, and called her blessed: her husband, and he praised her.

PROVERBS 31:10–12, 16–28

Blessed are all they that fear the Lord: that walk in his ways. For thou shalt eat the labours of thy hands: blessed art thou, and it shall be well with thee. Thy wife as a fruitful vine, on the sides of thy house. Thy children as olive plants, round about thy table. Behold, thus shall the man be blessed that feareth the Lord.

PSALM 124:1–4

Children, listen to me for I am your father: do what I tell you, and so be safe; for the Lord honors the father above his children and upholds the rights of a mother over her sons. Whoever respects a father expiates sins, whoever honors a mother is like someone amassing a fortune. Whoever respects a father will in turn be happy with children, the day he prays for help, he will be heard.

ECCLESIASTICUS 3:1–5 NJB

Hear, O Israel, the Lord our God is one Lord. Thou shalt love the Lord thy God with thy whole heart, and with thy whole soul, and with thy whole strength. And these words which I command thee this day, shall be in thy heart: And thou shalt tell them to thy children, and thou shalt meditate upon them sitting in thy house, and walking on thy journey, sleeping and rising. And thou shalt bind them as a sign on thy hand, and they shall be and shall move between thy eyes. And thou shalt write them in the entry, and on the doors of thy house.

DEUTERONOMY 6:4–9

Grandchildren are the crown of old men, and the glory of children is their parentage.

PROVERBS 17:6 NABRE

Fear

*n.: An unpleasant often strong emotion caused
by expectation or awareness of danger.*

Thus we do not fear, though earth be shaken and mountains quake to the depths of the sea, though its waters rage and foam and mountains totter at its surging. The Lord of hosts is with us; our stronghold is the God of Jacob. Selah.

PSALM 46:2–4 NABRE

Yahweh is my light and my salvation, whom should I fear? Yahweh is the fortress of my life, whom should I dread? When the wicked advance against me to eat me up, they, my opponents, my enemies, are the ones who stumble and fall. Though an army pitch camp against me, my heart will not fear, though war break out against me, my trust will never be shaken.

PSALM 27:1–3 NJB

Whosoever are led by the Spirit of God, they are the sons of God. For you have not received the spirit of bondage again in fear: but you have received the spirit of adoption of sons, whereby we cry: Abba (Father). For the Spirit himself giveth testimony to our spirit that we are the sons of God.

ROMANS 8:14–16

When I am afraid, I put my trust in you, in God, whose word I praise, in God I put my trust and have no fear, what power has human strength over me?

PSALM 56:3–4 NJB

He [God] hath said: I will not leave thee: neither will I forsake thee. So that we may confidently say: The Lord is my helper: I will not fear what man shall do to me.

HEBREWS 13:5–6

Even were I to walk in a ravine as dark as death I should fear no danger, for you are at my side. Your staff and your crook are there to soothe me.

Psalm 23:4 njb

Fear not, for I am with thee: turn not aside, for I am thy God: I have strengthened thee, and have helped thee, and the right hand of my just one hath upheld thee. Behold all that fight against thee shall be confounded and ashamed, they shall be as nothing, and the men shall perish that strive against thee. Thou shalt seek them, and shalt not find the men that resist thee: they shall be as nothing: and as a thing consumed the men that war against thee. For I am the Lord thy God, who take thee by the hand, and say to thee: Fear not, I have helped thee.

Isaias 41:10–13

Behold, God is my saviour, I will deal confidently, and will not fear: because the Lord is my strength, and my praise, and he is become my salvation.

Isaias 12:2

Let not your heart be troubled: nor let it be afraid. You have heard that I said to you: I go away, and I come unto you. If you loved me you would indeed be glad, because I go to the Father: for the Father is greater than I.

John 14:28

You shall not fear the terror of the night nor the arrow that flies by day, nor the pestilence that roams in darkness, nor the plague that ravages at noon. Though a thousand fall at your side, ten thousand at your right hand, near you it shall not come.

Psalm 91:5–7 nabre

Forgiveness

n.: The act of giving up resentment
of and pardoning an offender.

He commissioned us to preach to the people and testify that
he [Jesus] is the one appointed by God as judge of the living and the dead. To him all the prophets bear witness, that
everyone who believes in him will receive forgiveness of sins
through his name.

ACTS 10:42–43 NABRE

Giving thanks to God the Father, who hath made us worthy
to be partakers of the lot of the saints in light: Who hath
delivered us from the power of darkness and hath translated
us into the kingdom of the Son of his love, in whom we
have redemption through his blood, the remission of sins:

COLOSSIANS 1:12–14

If you will forgive men their offences, your heavenly Father
will forgive you also your offences. But if you will not forgive
men, neither will your Father forgive you your offences.

MATTHEW 6:14–15

If any one have caused grief, he hath not grieved me: but in
part, that I may not burden you all. To him who is such a one,
this rebuke is sufficient, which is given by many. So that on
the contrary, you should rather forgive him and comfort him,
lest perhaps such a one be swallowed up with overmuch sorrow. Wherefore, I beseech you that you would confirm your
charity towards him. For to this end also did I write, that I
may know the experiment of you, whether you be obedient in
all things. And to whom you have pardoned any thing, I also.
For, what I have pardoned, if I have pardoned any thing, for
your sakes have I done it in the person of Christ.

2 CORINTHIANS 2:5–10

Let all bitterness and anger and indignation and clamour and blasphemy be put away from you, with all malice. And be ye kind one to another: merciful, forgiving one another, even as God hath forgiven you in Christ.

EPHESIANS 4:31

He does not treat us as our sins deserve, nor repay us as befits our offences. As the height of heaven above earth, so strong is his faithful love for those who fear him. As the distance of east from west, so far from us does he put our faults. As tenderly as a father treats his children, so Yahweh treats those who fear him.

PSALM 103:10–13 NJB

Thou, O Lord, art good and forgiving, abounding in steadfast love to all who call on thee. Give ear, O Lord, to my prayer; hearken to my cry of supplication.

PSALM 86:5–6 RSV-CE

When you shall stand to pray, forgive, if you have aught against any man: that your Father also, who is in heaven, may forgive you your sins. But if you will not forgive, neither will your father that is in heaven forgive you your sins.

MARK 11:25–26

Put ye on therefore, as the elect of God, holy and beloved, the bowels of mercy, benignity, humility, modesty, patience: Bearing with one another and forgiving one another, if any have a complaint against another. Even as the Lord hath forgiven you, so do you also.

COLOSSIANS 3:12–13

If we say that we have no sin, we deceive ourselves and the truth is not in us. If we confess our sins, he is faithful and just, to forgive us our sins and to cleanse us from all iniquity.

1 JOHN 1:8–9

Freedom

n.: The quality or state of being without necessity,
coercion, or constraint in choice or action.

There is therefore now no condemnation for those who are
in Christ Jesus. For the law of the Spirit of life in Christ
Jesus has set me free from the law of sin and death. For God
has done what the law, weakened by the flesh, could not do:
sending his own Son in the likeness of sinful flesh and for
sin, he condemned sin in the flesh, in order that the just requirement of the law might be fulfilled in us, who walk not
according to the flesh but according to the Spirit.

ROMANS 8:1–4 RSV-CE

For creation awaits with eager expectation the revelation of
the children of God; for creation was made subject to futil-
ity, not of its own accord but because of the one who subjected it, in hope that creation itself would be set free from
slavery to corruption and share in the glorious freedom of
the children of God.

ROMANS 8:10–21 NABRE

Be free, yet without using freedom as a pretext for evil, but
as slaves of God. Give honor to all, love the community, fear
God, honor the king.

1 PETER 2:16–17 NABRE

Christ set us free, so that we should remain free. Stand firm,
then, and do not let yourselves be fastened again to the yoke
of slavery.

GALATIANS 5:1 NJB

Jesus said to those Jews who believed him: If you continue in my word, you shall be my disciples indeed. And you shall know the truth: and the truth shall make you free. Jesus answered them: Amen, amen, I say unto you that whosoever committeth sin is the servant of sin. Now the servant abideth not in the house for ever: but the son abideth for ever. If therefore the son shall make you free, you shall be free indeed.

JOHN 8:31–32, 34–36

Anyone who listens to the Word and takes no action is like someone who looks at his own features in a mirror and, once he has seen what he looks like, goes off and immediately forgets it. But anyone who looks steadily at the perfect law of freedom and keeps to it—not listening and forgetting, but putting it into practice—will be blessed in every undertaking.

JAMES 1:23–24 NJB

This Lord is the Spirit and where the Spirit of the Lord is, there is freedom. And all of us, with our unveiled faces like mirrors reflecting the glory of the Lord, are being transformed into the image that we reflect in brighter and brighter glory; this is the working of the Lord who is the Spirit.

2 CORINTHIANS 3:17–18 NJB

The maker of heaven and earth, the seas and all that is in them, Who keeps faith forever, secures justice for the oppressed, gives food to the hungry. The Lord sets prisoners free; the Lord gives sight to the blind.

PSALM 146:6–8 NABRE

Friendship

n.: The state of being attached to
another by affection or esteem.

A faithful friend is a sturdy shelter; he who finds one finds a
treasure. A faithful friend is beyond price, no sum can balance
his worth. A faithful friend is a life-saving remedy, such as he
who fears God finds; For he who fears God behaves accord-
ingly, and his friend will be like himself.

SIRACH 6:14–16 NABRE

He that is a friend loveth at all times: and a brother is
proved in distress.

PROVERBS 17:17

Better are the wounds of a friend, than the deceitful kisses of
an enemy. A soul that is full shall tread upon the honeycomb:
and a soul that is hungry shall take even bitter for sweet. As a
bird that wandereth from her nest, so is a man that leaveth his
place. Ointment and perfumes rejoice the heart: and the good
counsels of a friend are sweet to the soul. Thy own friend, and
thy father's friend, forsake not: and go not into thy brother's
house in the day of thy affliction. Better is a neighbour that is
near than a brother afar off.

PROVERBS 27:6, 9–10

Greater love than this no man hath, that a man lay down his
life for his friends. You are my friends, if you do the things
that I command you. I will not now call you servants: for the
servant knoweth not what his lord doth. But I have called
you friends. Because all things, whatsoever I have heard of
my Father, I have made known to you.

JOHN 15:13–15

It is better therefore that two should be together, than one: for they have the advantage of their society: If one fall he shall be supported by the other: woe to him that is alone, for when he falleth, he hath none to lift him up. And if two lie together, they shall warm one another: how shall one alone be warmed? And if a man prevail against one, two shall withstand him.

ECCLESIASTES 4:9–12

He that neglecteth a loss for the sake of a friend, is just: but the way of the wicked shall deceive them.

PROVERBS 12:26

Some friends bring ruin on us, but a true friend is more loyal than a brother.

PROVERBS 18:24 NABRE

Love one another with mutual affection; anticipate one another in showing honor.

ROMANS 12:10 NABRE

At midnight I rise to praise you for your upright judgments. I am a friend to all who fear you and keep your precepts. Your faithful love fills the earth, Yahweh, teach me your judgments.

PSALM 119:62–64 NJB

The scripture was fulfilled, saying: Abraham believed God, and it was reputed to him to justice, and he was called the friend of God.

JAMES 2:23

He that walketh with the wise, shall be wise: a friend of fools shall become like to them.

PROVERBS 13:20

Fruit of the Spirit

n.: Those gracious habits produced in the life
of a Christian as a result of the indwelling
of the Holy Spirit.

The parable is this: The seed is the word of God. And they by the way side are they that hear: then the devil cometh and taketh the word out of their heart, lest believing they should be saved. Now they upon the rock are they who when they hear receive the word with joy: and these have no roots: for they believe for a while and in time of temptation they fall away. And that which fell among thorns are they who have heard and, going their way, are choked with the cares and riches and pleasures of this life and yield no fruit. But that on the good ground are they who in a good and perfect heart, hearing the word, keep it and bring forth fruit in patience.

LUKE 8:11–15

Blessed is the man who hath not walked in the counsel of the ungodly, nor stood in the way of sinners, nor sat in the chair of pestilence: But his will is in the law of the Lord, and on his law he shall meditate day and night. And he shall be like a tree which is planted near the running waters, which shall bring forth its fruit, in due season. And his leaf shall not fall off: and all whatsoever he shall do shall prosper.

PSALM 1:1–3

This I pray: That your charity may more and more abound in knowledge and in all understanding: That you may approve the better things: that you may be sincere and without offence unto the day of Christ: Filled with the fruit of justice, through Jesus Christ, unto the glory and praise of God.

PHILIPPIANS 1:9–11

We always give thanks to God, the Father of our Lord Jesus Christ, when we pray for you, for we have heard of your faith in Christ Jesus and the love that you have for all the holy ones because of the hope reserved for you in heaven. Of this you have already heard through the word of truth, the gospel, that has come to you. Just as in the whole world it is bearing fruit and growing, so also among you, from the day you heard it and came to know the grace of God in truth.

COLOSSIANS 1:3–6 NABRE

Make every effort to supplement your faith with virtue, virtue with knowledge, knowledge with self-control, self-control with endurance, endurance with devotion, devotion with mutual affection, mutual affection with love. If these are yours and increase in abundance, they will keep you from being idle or unfruitful in the knowledge of our Lord Jesus Christ.

2 PETER 1:5–8 NABRE

Live in a manner worthy of the Lord, so as to be fully pleasing, in every good work bearing fruit and growing in the knowledge of God, strengthened with every power, in accord with his glorious might, for all endurance and patience, with joy giving thanks to the Father, who has made you fit to share in the inheritance of the holy ones in light.

COLOSSIANS 1:10–12 NABRE

Generosity
n.: Liberality in spirit or action.

I am old, but ever since my youth I never saw an upright person abandoned, or the descendants of the upright forced to beg their bread. The upright is always compassionate, always lending, so his descendants reap a blessing.

Psalm 37:25–26 NJB

All goes well for those gracious in lending, who conduct their affairs with justice. They shall never be shaken; the just shall be remembered forever. They shall not fear an ill report; their hearts are steadfast, trusting the Lord. Their hearts are tranquil, without fear, till at last they look down on their foes. Lavishly they give to the poor; their prosperity shall endure forever; their horn shall be exalted in honor.

Psalm 112:5–9 NABRE

He who soweth sparingly shall also reap sparingly: and he who soweth in blessings shall also reap blessings. Every one as he hath determined in his heart, not with sadness or of necessity: for God loveth a cheerful giver. And God is able to make all grace abound in you: that ye always, having all sufficiently in all things, may abound to every good work.

2 Corinthians 9:6–8

Give: and it shall be given to you: good measure and pressed down and shaken together and running over shall they give into your bosom. For with the same measure that you shall mete withal, it shall be measured to you again.

Luke 6:38

Whosoever shall give you to drink a cup of water in my name, because you belong to Christ: amen I say to you, he shall not lose his reward.

Mark 9:40

As it is written: He hath dispersed abroad, he hath given to the poor: his justice remaineth for ever. And he that ministereth seed to the sower will both give you bread to eat and will multiply your seed and increase the growth of the fruits of your justice.

2 CORINTHIANS 9:9–10

One man gives freely, yet grows all the richer; another withholds what he should give, and only suffers want. A liberal man will be enriched, and one who waters will himself be watered.

PROVERBS 11:24–25 RSV-CE

He who has a bountiful eye will be blessed, for he shares his bread with the poor.

PROVERBS 22:9 RSV-CE

Is there anyone poor among you, one of your brothers, in any town of yours in the country which Yahweh your God is giving you? Do not harden your heart or close your hand against that poor brother of yours, but be open handed with him and lend him enough for his needs.

DEUTERONOMY 15:7–8 NJB

By every means I have shown you that we must exert ourselves in this way to support the weak, remembering the words of the Lord Jesus, who himself said, "There is more happiness in giving than in receiving."

ACTS 20:35 NJB

You shall give to him freely, and your heart shall not be grudging when you give to him; because for this the Lord your God will bless you in all your work and in all that you undertake. For the poor will never cease out of the land; therefore I command you, You shall open wide your hand to your brother, to the needy and to the poor, in the land.

DEUTERONOMY 15:10–11 RSV-CE

Gentleness

n.: The state of being mild, docile,
soft, or moderate; not harsh.

Your adornment should not be an external one: braiding the hair, wearing gold jewelry, or dressing in fine clothes, but rather the hidden character of the heart, expressed in the imperishable beauty of a gentle and calm disposition, which is precious in the sight of God. For this is also how the holy women who hoped in God once used to adorn themselves and were subordinate to their husbands.

1 PETER 3:3–5 NABRE

The fruit of the Spirit is love, joy, peace, patience, kindness, generosity, faithfulness, gentleness, self-control. Against such there is no law. Now those who belong to Christ (Jesus) have crucified their flesh with its passions and desires. If we live in the Spirit, let us also follow the Spirit.

GALATIANS 5:22–25 NABRE

The love of money is the root of all evils, and some people in their desire for it have strayed from the faith and have pierced themselves with many pains. But, you, man of God, avoid all this. Instead, pursue righteousness, devotion, faith, love, patience, and gentleness.

1 TIMOTHY 6:10–11 NABRE

In your hearts reverence Christ as Lord. Always be prepared to make a defense to any one who calls you to account for the hope that is in you, yet do it with gentleness and reverence.

1 PETER 3:15 RSV-CE

Come to me, all who labor and are heavy laden, and I will give you rest. Take my yoke upon you, and learn from me; for I am gentle and lowly in heart, and you will find rest for your souls. For my yoke is easy, and my burden is light.

MATTHEW 11:28–30 RSV-CE

Admonish them to be subject to princes and powers, to obey at a word, to be ready to every good work. To speak evil of no man, not to be litigious but gentle: shewing all mildness towards all men.

TITUS 3:1–2

I, the prisoner in the Lord, urge you therefore to lead a life worthy of the vocation to which you were called. With all humility and gentleness, and with patience, support each other in love.

EPHESIANS 4:1–2 NJB

As the chosen of God, then, the holy people whom he loves, you are to be clothed in heartfelt compassion, in generosity and humility, gentleness and patience.

COLOSSIANS 3:12 NJB

If any one aspires to the office of bishop, he desires a noble task. Now a bishop must be above reproach, the husband of one wife, temperate, sensible, dignified, hospitable, an apt teacher, no drunkard, not violent but gentle, not quarrelsome, and no lover of money.

1 TIMOTHY 3:1–3 RSV-CE

The Lord's servant must not be quarrelsome but kindly to every one, an apt teacher, forbearing, correcting his opponents with gentleness. God may perhaps grant that they will repent and come to know the truth.

2 TIMOTHY 2:24–25 RSV-CE

God's Will

n.: An outline or blueprint of God's intention
for you instituted at the time He created you.

I know well the plans I have in mind for you, says the Lord,
plans for your welfare, not for woe! plans to give you a future
full of hope. When you call me, when you go to pray to me,
I will listen to you. When you look for me, you will find me.
Yes, when you seek me with all your heart.

JEREMIAH 29:11–13 NABRE

That he [God] might make known unto us the mystery of
his will, according to his good pleasure, which he hath purposed in him, in the dispensation of the fulness of times, to
re-establish all things in Christ, that are in heaven and on
earth, in him. In whom we also are called by lot, being predestinated according to the purpose of him who worketh all
things according to the counsel of his will. That we may be
unto the praise of his glory: we who before hoped in Christ.

EPHESIANS 1:9–12

All that the Father giveth to me shall come to me: and him
that cometh to me, I will not cast out. Because I came down
from heaven, not to do my own will but the will of him that
sent me. Now this is the will of the Father who sent me:
that of all that he hath given me, I should lose nothing; but
should raise it up again in the last day. And this is the will of
my Father that sent me: that every one who seeth the Son
and believeth in him may have life everlasting. And I will
raise him up in the last day.

JOHN 6:37–40

We also, from the day that we heard it, cease not to pray for you and to beg that you may be filled with the knowledge of his will, in all wisdom and spiritual understanding: that you may walk worthy of God, in all things pleasing; being fruitful in every good work and increasing in the knowledge of God.

COLOSSIANS 1:9–10

In [Christ] whom we also are called by lot, being predestinated according to the purpose of him who worketh all things according to the counsel of his will. That we may be unto the praise of his glory: we who before hoped in Christ.

EPHESIANS 1:11–12 RSV-CE

This is the confidence which we have towards him: that, whatsoever we shall ask according to his will, he heareth us. And we know that he heareth us whatsoever we ask: we know that we have the petitions which we request of him.

1 JOHN 5:14–15

I beseech you therefore, brethren, by the mercy of God, that you present your bodies a living sacrifice, holy, pleasing unto God, your reasonable service. And be not conformed to this world: but be reformed in the newness of your mind, that you may prove what is the good and the acceptable and the perfect will of God.

ROMANS 12:1–2

Brethren, I do not count myself to have apprehended. But one thing I do: Forgetting the things that are behind and stretching forth myself to those that are before, I press towards the mark, to the prize of the supernal vocation of God in Christ Jesus.

PHILIPPIANS 3:13–14

Goodness
n.: The state of being good.

Let us not grow tired of doing good, for in due time we shall reap our harvest, if we do not give up. So then, while we have the opportunity, let us do good to all, but especially to those who belong to the family of the faith.

Galatians 6:9–10 nabre

Be subject to every human institution for the Lord's sake, whether it be to the king as supreme or to governors as sent by him for the punishment of evildoers and the approval of those who do good. For it is the will of God that by doing good you may silence the ignorance of foolish people.

1 Peter 2:13–15 nabre

Let us consider one another, to provoke unto charity and to good works: Not forsaking our assembly, as some are accustomed: but comforting one anther, and so much the more as you see the day approaching.

Hebrews 10:24–25

How great is your goodness, Lord, stored up for those who fear you. You display it for those who trust you, in the sight of all the people. You hide them in the shelter of your presence, safe from scheming enemies. You keep them in your abode, safe from plotting tongues.

Psalm 31:20–21

Behold one came and said to him: Good master, what good shall I do that I may have life everlasting? Who said to him: Why askest thou me concerning good? One is good, God. But if thou wilt enter into life, keep the commandments.

Matthew 19:16–17

Beloved, I urge you as aliens and sojourners to keep away from worldly desires that wage war against the soul. Maintain good conduct among the Gentiles, so that if they speak of you as evildoers, they may observe your good works and glorify God on the day of visitation.

1 PETER 2:11–12 NABRE

Every creature of God is good, and nothing to be rejected that is received with thanksgiving: for it is sanctified by the word of God and prayer. These things proposing to the brethren, thou shalt be a good minister of Christ Jesus, nourished up in the words of faith and of the good doctrine which thou hast attained unto.

1 TIMOTHY 4:4–6

In all things shew thyself an example of good works, in doctrine, in integrity, in gravity, The sound word that can not be blamed: that he who is on the contrary part may be afraid, having no evil to say of us.

TITUS 2:7–8

Hearing of thy charity and faith, which thou hast in the Lord Jesus and towards all the saints: That the communication of thy faith may be made evident in the acknowledgment of every good work that is in you in Christ Jesus. For I have had great joy and consolation in thy charity, because the bowels of the saints have been refreshed by thee, brother.

PHILEMON 1:5–7

It is a faithful saying. And these things I will have thee affirm constantly, that they who believe in God may be careful to excel in good works. These things are good and profitable unto men.

TITUS 3:8

Grace

*n.: Undeserved favor from God based
on someone else's worthiness.*

God (who is rich in mercy) for his exceeding charity wherewith he loved us even when we were dead in sins, hath
quickened us together in Christ (by whose grace you are
saved) and hath raised us up together and hath made us sit
together in the heavenly places, through Christ Jesus, that he
might shew in the ages to come the abundant riches of his
grace, in his bounty towards us in Christ Jesus. For by grace
you are saved through faith: and that not of yourselves, for it
is the gift of God. Not of works, that no man may glory.

EPHESIANS 2:4–9

I give thanks to my God always for you, for the grace of
God that is given you in Christ Jesus: that in all things you
are made rich in him, in all utterance and in all knowledge;
as the testimony of Christ was confirmed in you, so that
nothing is wanting to you in any grace, waiting for the manifestation of our Lord Jesus Christ.

1 CORINTHIANS 1:4–7

When the kindness and love of God our Saviour for hu-
manity were revealed, it was not because of any upright actions we had done ourselves; it was for no reason except his
own faithful love that he saved us, by means of the cleansing
water of rebirth and renewal in the Holy Spirit which he has
so generously poured over us through Jesus Christ our Saviour; so that, justified by his grace, we should become heirs
in hope of eternal life.

TITUS 3:4–7 NJB

If, by the transgression of one person, death came to reign through that one, how much more will those who receive the abundance of grace and of the gift of justification come to reign in life through the one person Jesus Christ. In conclusion, just as through one transgression condemnation came upon all, so through one righteous act acquittal and life came to all. For just as through the disobedience of one person the many were made sinners, so through the obedience of one the many will be made righteous. The law entered in so that transgression might increase but, where sin increased, grace overflowed all the more, so that, as sin reigned in death, grace also might reign through justification for eternal life through Jesus Christ our Lord.

ROMANS 5:17–21 NABRE

John testified to him and cried out, saying, "This was he of whom I said, 'The one who is coming after me ranks ahead of me because he existed before me.'" From his fullness we have all received, grace in place of grace, because while the law was given through Moses, grace and truth came through Jesus Christ.

JOHN 1:15–17 NABRE

Gird up your minds, be sober, set your hope fully upon the grace that is coming to you at the revelation of Jesus Christ.

1 PETER 1:13 RSV-CE

God resisteth the proud and giveth grace to the humble. Be subject therefore to God. But resist the devil: and he will fly from you. Draw nigh to God: and he will draw nigh to you.

JAMES 4:6–8

To every one of us is given grace, according to the measure of the giving of Christ.

EPHESIANS 4:7

Guidance

n.: The act of leading or directing
another on a course.

If you bestow your bread on the hungry and satisfy the afflicted; Then light shall rise for you in the darkness, and the gloom shall become for you like midday; then the Lord will guide you always and give you plenty even on the parched land. He will renew your strength, and you shall be like a watered garden, like a spring whose water never fails.

ISAIAH 58:10–11 NABRE

Keep your father's precept, my child, do not spurn your mother's teaching. Bind them ever to your heart, tie them round your neck. While you are active, they will guide you, when you fall asleep, they will watch over you, when you wake up, they will converse with you. For the precept is a lamp, the teaching is a light; correction and discipline are the way to life.

PROVERBS 6:20–23 NJB

Direct me in your ways, Yahweh, and teach me your paths. Encourage me to walk in your truth and teach me since you are the God who saves me. For my hope is in you all day long—such is your generosity, Yahweh.

PSALM 25:4–5 NJB

I stretch out my hands to thee; my soul thirsts for thee like a parched land. [Selah] Make haste to answer me, O Lord! My spirit fails! Hide not thy face from me, lest I be like those who go down to the Pit. Let me hear in the morning of thy steadfast love, for in thee I put my trust. Teach me the way I should go, for to thee I lift up my soul.

PSALM 143:6–8 RSV-CE

In you, Yahweh, I have taken refuge, let me never be put to shame, in your saving justice deliver me, rescue me, turn your ear to me, make haste. Be for me a rock-fastness, a fortified citadel to save me. You are my rock, my rampart; true to your name, lead me and guide me!

PSALM 31:1–3 NJB

When the Spirit of truth comes, he will guide you into all the truth; for he will not speak on his own authority, but whatever he hears he will speak, and he will declare to you the things that are to come.

JOHN 16:13 RSV-CE

Have confidence in the Lord with all thy heart, and lean not upon thy own prudence. In all thy ways think on him, and he will direct thy steps.

PROVERBS 3:5–6

That men may appreciate wisdom and discipline, may understand words of intelligence; May receive training in wise conduct, in what is right, just and honest; that resourcefulness may be imparted to the simple, to the young man knowledge and discretion. A wise man by hearing them [the proverbs of Solomon] will advance in learning, an intelligent man will gain sound guidance, that he may comprehend proverb and parable, the words of the wise and their riddles.

PROVERBS 1:2–6 NABRE

I stayed in your presence, you grasped me by the right hand; you will guide me with advice, and will draw me in the wake of your glory.

PSALM 73:23–24 NJB

Guilt

*n.: The state of deserving blame or a feeling
of responsibility for offenses.*

I make no secret of my guilt, I am anxious at the thought of
my sin. There is no numbering those who oppose me without cause, no counting those who hate me unprovoked, re-
paying me evil for good, slandering me for trying to do them
good. Yahweh, do not desert me, my God, do not stand aloof
from me. Come quickly to my help, Lord, my Saviour!

PSALM 38:18–22 NJB

My sins stand higher than my head, they weigh on me as
an unbearable weight. I have stinking, festering wounds,
thanks to my folly. I am twisted and bent double, I spend
my days in gloom. My loins burn with fever, no part of me is
unscathed. Numbed and utterly crushed I groan in distress
of heart. Lord, all my longing is known to you, my sighing
no secret from you, my heart is throbbing, my strength has
failed, the light has gone out of my eyes. For in you, Yahweh,
I put my hope, you, Lord my God, will give answer.

PSALM 38:4–10, 15 NJB

When you stretch out your hands I turn my eyes away. You
may multiply your prayers, I shall not be listening. Your hands
are covered in blood, wash, make yourselves clean. Take your
wrong-doing out of my sight. Cease doing evil. Learn to do
good, search for justice, discipline the violent, be just to the
orphan, plead for the widow. "Come, let us talk this over," says
Yahweh. "Though your sins are like scarlet, they shall be white
as snow; though they are red as crimson, they shall be like
wool."

ISAIAH 1:15–18 NJB

Who can discern his errors? Clear thou me from hidden faults. Keep back thy servant also from presumptuous sins; let them not have dominion over me! Then I shall be blameless, and innocent of great transgression.

PSALM 19:12–13 RSV-CE

I have formed thee, thou art my servant, O Israel, forget me not. I have blotted out thy iniquities as a cloud, and thy sins as a mist: return to me, for I have redeemed thee. Give praise, O ye heavens, for the Lord hath shewn mercy: shout with joy, ye ends of the earth: ye mountains, resound with praise, thou, O forest, and every tree therein.

ISAIAS 44:21–23

How blessed are those whose offence is forgiven, whose sin blotted out. How blessed are those to whom Yahweh imputes no guilt, whose spirit harbors no deceit. I said not a word, but my bones wasted away from groaning all the day; day and night your hand lay heavy upon me; my heart grew parched as stubble in summer drought. Pause. I made my sin known to you, did not conceal my guilt. I said, "I shall confess my offence to Yahweh." And you, for your part, took away my guilt, forgave my sin. Pause.

PSALM 32:1–5 NJB

The Lord declares: In their minds I shall plant my laws writing them on their hearts. Then I shall be their God, and they shall be my people. There will be no further need for each to teach his neighbour, and each his brother, saying "Learn to know the Lord!" No, they will all know me, from the least to the greatest, since I shall forgive their guilt and never more call their sins to mind.

HEBREWS 8:10–12 NJB

Health & Healing

*n.: The condition of being sound in
body and mind or the act of being
made sound in body or mind.*

He [Jesus] himself bore our sins in his body upon the cross,
so that, free from sin, we might live for righteousness. By his
wounds you have been healed.

1 Peter 2:24 nabre

Despised, and the most abject of men, a man of sorrows, and
acquainted with infirmity: and his look was as it were hidden and despised, whereupon we esteemed him not. Surely
he hath borne our infirmities and carried our sorrows: and
we have thought him as it were a leper, and as one struck by
God and afflicted. But he was wounded for our iniquities, he
was bruised for our sins: the chastisement of our peace was
upon him, and by his bruises we are healed.

Isaias 53:3–5

Is any man sick among you? Let him bring in the priests of
the church, and let them pray over him, anointing him with
oil in the name of the Lord. And the prayer of faith shall
save the sick man: and the Lord shall raise him up: and if he
be in sins, they shall be forgiven him.

James 5:14–15

God anointed him [Jesus of Nazareth] with the Holy
Ghost, and with power, who went about doing good, and
healing all that were oppressed by the devil, for God was
with him. And we are witnesses of all things that he did in
the land of the Jews and in Jerusalem, whom they killed,
hanging him upon a tree.

Acts 10:38–39

These signs shall follow them that believe: In my name they shall cast out devils: they shall speak with new tongues. They shall take up serpents; and if they shall drink any deadly thing, it shall not hurt them: they shall lay their hands upon the sick, and they shall recover.

MARK 16:17–18

Some were sick through their sinful ways, and because of their iniquities suffered affliction; they loathed any kind of food, and they drew near to the gates of death. Then they cried to the Lord in their trouble, and he delivered them from their distress; he sent forth his word, and healed them, and delivered them from destruction. Let them thank the Lord for his steadfast love, for his wonderful works to the sons of men!

PSALM 107:17–21 RSV-CE

Bless Yahweh, my soul, from the depths of my being, his holy name; bless Yahweh, my soul, never forget all his acts of kindness. He forgives all your offences, cures all your diseases, he redeems your life from the abyss, crowns you with faithful love and tenderness; he contents you with good things all your life, renews your youth like an eagle's.

PSALM 103:1–5 NJB

You will worship Yahweh your God, and then I shall bless your food and water, and keep you free of sickness.

EXODUS 23:25 NJB

If thou wilt hear the voice of the Lord thy God, and do what is right before him, and obey his commandments, and keep all his precepts, none of the evils that I laid upon Egypt, will I bring upon thee: for I am the Lord thy healer.

EXODUS 15:26

Heaven

*n.: A place of everlasting communion
with God after death.*

Let not your heart be troubled. You believe in God, believe
also in me. In my Father's house there are many mansions.
If not, I would have told you: because I go to prepare a place
for you. And if I shall go, and prepare a place for you, I will
come again, and will take you to myself; that where I am,
you also may be.

JOHN 14:1–3

Blessed are ye when they shall revile you, and persecute you,
and speak all that is evil against you, untruly, for my sake: Be
glad and rejoice, for your reward is very great in heaven.

MATTHEW 5:11–12

Lay not up to yourselves treasures on earth: where the rust,
and moth consume, and where thieves break through and
steal. But lay up to yourselves treasures in heaven: where neither the rust nor moth doth consume, and where thieves do
not break through, nor steal. For where thy treasure is, there
is thy heart also.

MATTHEW 6:19–21

Our commonwealth is in heaven, and from it we await a
Savior, the Lord Jesus Christ, who will change our lowly
body to be like his glorious body, by the power which en-
ables him even to subject all things to himself.

PHILIPPIANS 3:20–21 RSV-CE

We look for new heavens and a new earth according to his
promises, in which justice dwelleth. Wherefore, dearly beloved, waiting for these things, be diligent that you may be
found before him unspotted and blameless in peace.

2 PETER 3:13–14

Blessed be the God and Father of our Lord Jesus Christ, who according to his great mercy hath regenerated us unto a lively hope, by the resurrection of Jesus Christ from the dead, Unto an inheritance incorruptible, and undefiled, and that can not fade, reserved in heaven for you, Who, by the power of God, are kept by faith unto salvation, ready to be revealed in the last time.

1 PETER 1:3–5

We speak the wisdom of God in a mystery, a wisdom which is hidden, which God ordained before the world, unto our glory: Which none of the princes of this world knew; for if they had known it, they would never have crucified the Lord of glory. But, as it is written: That eye hath not seen, nor ear heard, neither hath it entered into the heart of man, what things God hath prepared for them that love him.

1 CORINTHIANS 2:7–9

I tell you, there will be more rejoicing in heaven over one sinner repenting than over ninety-nine upright people who have no need of repentance.

LUKE 15:7 NJB

Seeing the crowds, he went up on the mountain, and when he sat down his disciples came to him. And he opened his mouth and taught them, saying: "Blessed are the poor in spirit, for theirs is the kingdom of heaven."

MATTHEW 5:1–3 RSV-CE

I saw a new heaven and a new earth. For the first heaven and the first earth was gone, and the sea is now no more. And I John saw the holy city, the new Jerusalem, coming down out of heaven from God, prepared as a bride adorned for her husband.

REVELATION 21:1–2

Holiness

n.: The state of being perfect in goodness.

As obedient children, do not be conformed to the passions
of your former ignorance, but as he who called you is holy,
be holy yourselves in all your conduct; since it is written,
"You shall be holy, for I am holy."

1 PETER 1:14–16 RSV-CE

All the gods of the nations are idols: but the Lord made the
heavens. Praise and magnificence are before him: strength
and joy in his place. Bring ye to the Lord, O ye families of
the nations: bring ye to the Lord glory and empire. Give to
the Lord glory to his name, bring up sacrifice, and come ye
in his sight: and adore the Lord in holy becomingness. Let
all the earth be moved at his presence: for he hath founded
the world immoveable.

1 CHRONICLES 16:26–30

My heart hath rejoiced in the Lord, and my horn is exalted
in my God: my mouth is enlarged over my enemies: because
I have joyed in thy salvation. There is none holy as the Lord
is: for there is no other beside thee, and there is none strong
like our God.

1 SAMUEL 2:1–2

He chose us in him before the foundation of the world,
that we should be holy and unspotted in his sight in charity.
Who hath predestinated us unto the adoption of children
through Jesus Christ unto himself: according to the purpose
of his will.

EPHESIANS 1:4–5

Thus says the Lord God: I will show my greatness and my holiness and make myself known in the eyes of many nations. Then they will know that I am the Lord.

EZEKIEL 38:17, 23 RSV-CE

We have had earthly fathers to discipline us and we respected them. Shall we not much more be subject to the Father of spirits and live? For they disciplined us for a short time at their pleasure, but he disciplines us for our good, that we may share his holiness.

HEBREWS 12:9–10 RSV-CE

Strive for peace with all men, and for the holiness without which no one will see the Lord.

HEBREWS 12:14 RSV-CE

What manner of people ought you to be in holy conversation and godliness? Looking for and hasting unto the coming of the day of the Lord, by which the heavens being on fire shall be dissolved, and the elements shall melt with the burning heat? But we look for new heavens and a new earth according to his promises, in which justice dwelleth. Wherefore, dearly beloved, waiting for these things, be diligent that you may be found before him unspotted and blameless in peace.

2 PETER 3:11–14

May the Lord multiply you, and make you abound in charity towards one another, and towards all men: as we do also towards you, To confirm your hearts without blame, in holiness, before God and our Father, at the coming of our Lord Jesus Christ, with all his saints. Amen.

1 THESSALONIANS 3:12–13

Holy Spirit
n.: The Spirit of God.

If you ask anything in my name, I will do it. "If you love me, you will keep my commandments. And I will pray the Father, and he will give you another Counselor, to be with you for ever, even the Spirit of truth, whom the world cannot receive, because it neither sees him nor knows him; you know him, for he dwells with you, and will be in you."

JOHN 14:14–17 RSV-CE

In the same way, the Spirit too comes to the aid of our weakness; for we do not know how to pray as we ought, but the Spirit itself intercedes with inexpressible groanings. And the one who searches hearts knows what is the intention of the Spirit, because it intercedes for the holy ones according to God's will.

ROMANS 8:26–27 NABRE

The Holy Ghost also doth testify this to us. For after that he said: and this is the testament which I will make unto them after those days, saith the Lord. I will give my laws in their hearts and on their minds will I write them: and their sins and iniquities I will remember no more.

HEBREWS 10:15–17

I will ask the Father, and he will give you another Advocate to be with you always, the Spirit of truth, which the world cannot accept, because it neither sees nor knows it. But you know it, because it remains with you, and will be in you.

JOHN 14:16–17 NABRE

The Advocate, the holy Spirit that the Father will send in my name—he will teach you everything and remind you of all that (I) told you.

JOHN 14:26 NABRE

It shall come to pass afterward, that I will pour out my spirit on all flesh; your sons and your daughters shall prophesy, your old men shall dream dreams, and your young men shall see visions. Even upon the menservants and maidservants in those days, I will pour out my spirit.

Joel 2:28–29 rsv-ce

Peter said to them: Do penance: and be baptized every one of you in the name of Jesus Christ, for the remission of your sins. And you shall receive the gift of the Holy Ghost. For the promise is to you and to your children and to all that are far off, whomsoever the Lord our God shall call.

Acts 2:38–39

We have received not the spirit of this world, but the Spirit that is of God: that we may know the things that are given us from God. Which things also we speak: not in the learned words of human wisdom, but in the doctrine of the Spirit, comparing spiritual things with spiritual. But the sensual man perceiveth not these things that are of the Spirit of God. For it is foolishness to him: and he cannot understand, because it is spiritually examined. But the spiritual man judgeth all things: and he himself is judged of no man.

1 Corinthians 2:12–15

You too, in him, have heard the message of the truth and the gospel of your salvation, and having put your trust in it you have been stamped with the seal of the Holy Spirit of the promise, who is the pledge of our inheritance, for the freedom of the people whom God has taken for his own, for the praise of his glory.

Ephesians 1:13–14 njb

Hope

*n.: Desire accompanied by expectation
of or belief in fulfillment.*

It is he that giveth strength to the weary, and increaseth force and might to them that are not. Youths shall faint, and labour, and young men shall fall by infirmity. But they that hope in the Lord shall renew their strength, they shall take wings as eagles, they shall run and not be weary, they shall walk and not faint.

Isaias 40:29–31

These things I shall think over in my heart, therefore will I hope. The mercies of the Lord that we are not consumed: because his commiserations have not failed. They are new every morning, great is thy faithfulness. The Lord is my portion, said my soul: therefore will I wait for him. The Lord is good to them that hope in him, to the soul that seeketh him.

Lamentations 3:21–25

When God desired to show more convincingly to the heirs of the promise the unchangeable character of his purpose, he interposed with an oath, so that through two unchangeable things, in which it is impossible that God should prove false, we who have fled for refuge might have strong encouragement to seize the hope set before us. We have this as a sure and steadfast anchor of the soul, a hope that enters into the inner shrine behind the curtain, where Jesus has gone as a forerunner on our behalf.

Hebrews 6:17–20 rsv-ce

We labor and are reviled, because we hope in the living God, who is the Saviour of all men, especially of the faithful.

1 Timothy 4:10

In hope we were saved. Now hope that sees for itself is not hope. For who hopes for what one sees? But if we hope for what we do not see, we wait with endurance.

Romans 8:24–25 nabre

Brethren, stand fast; and hold the traditions which you have learned, whether by word, or by our epistle. Now our Lord Jesus Christ himself, and God and our Father, who hath loved us, and hath given us everlasting consolation, and good hope in grace, Exhort your hearts, and confirm you in every good work and word.

2 Thessalonians 2:14–16

For the grace of God our Saviour hath appeared to all men; instructing us, that, denying ungodliness and worldly desires, we should live soberly, and justly, and godly in this world, looking for the blessed hope and coming of the glory of the great God and our Saviour Jesus Christ, who gave himself for us, that he might redeem us from all iniquity, and might cleanse to himself a people acceptable, a pursuer of good works. These things speak, and exhort and rebuke with all authority. Let no man despise thee.

Titus 2:11–15

Blessed be the God and Father of our Lord Jesus Christ, who according to his great mercy hath regenerated us unto a lively hope, by the resurrection of Jesus Christ from the dead.

1 Peter 1:3

Humility

n.: The state of being modest
or meek in spirit or manner.

At that hour the disciples came to Jesus, saying: Who thinkest thou is the greater in the kingdom of heaven? And Jesus calling unto him a little child, set him in the midst of them, And said: Amen I say to you, unless you be converted, and become as little children, you shall not enter into the kingdom of heaven. Whosoever therefore shall humble himself as this little child, he is the greater in the kingdom of heaven.

MATTHEW 18:1–4

He that yieldeth to reproof possesseth understanding. The fear of the Lord is the lesson of wisdom: and humility goeth before glory.

PROVERBS 15:32–33

He that is the greatest among you shall be your servant. And whosoever shall exalt himself shall be humbled: and he that shall humble himself shall be exalted.

MATTHEW 23:11–12

Let nothing be done through contention, neither by vain glory: but in humility, let each esteem others better than themselves: Each one not considering the things that are his own, but those that are other men's. For let this mind be in you, which was also in Christ Jesus: Who being in the form of God, thought it not robbery to be equal with God: But emptied himself, taking the form of a servant, being made in the likeness of men, and in habit found as a man. He humbled himself, becoming obedient unto death, even to the death of the cross.

PHILIPPIANS 2:3–8

A deceitful balance is an abomination before the Lord: and a just weight is his will. Where pride is, there also shall be reproach: but where humility is, there also is wisdom. The simplicity of the just shall guide them.

PROVERBS 11:1–3

Pride goeth before destruction: and the spirit is lifted up before a fall. It is better to be humbled with the meek, than to divide spoils with the proud.

PROVERBS 16:18–19

In like manner, ye young men, be subject to the ancients. And do you all insinuate humility one to another, for God resisteth the proud, but to the humble he giveth grace. Be you humbled therefore under the mighty hand of God, that he may exalt you in the time of visitation: Casting all your care upon him, for he hath care of you.

1 PETER 5:5–7

He [God] giveth greater grace. Wherefore he saith: God resisteth the proud, and giveth grace to the humble. Be subject therefore to God. Be humbled in the sight of the Lord, and he will exalt you.

JAMES 4:6–7, 10

Praise the Lord! Sing to the Lord a new song, his praise in the assembly of the faithful! For the Lord takes pleasure in his people; he adorns the humble with victory.

PSALM 149:1, 4 RSV-CE

Humiliation followeth the proud: and glory shall uphold the humble of spirit.

PROVERBS 29:23

Instruction

n.: A precept, command, or order.

Direct me in your ways, Yahweh, and teach me your paths. Encourage me to walk in your truth and teach me since you are the God who saves me. For my hope is in you all day long such is your generosity, Yahweh.

PSALM 25:4–5 NJB

Take hold on instruction, leave it not: keep it, because it is thy life.

WISDOM 4:13

Keep the commandments of thy father, and forsake not the law of thy mother. Bind them in thy heart continually, and put them about thy neck. When thou walkest, let them go with thee: when thou sleepest, let them keep thee, and when thou awakest, talk with them. Because the commandment is a lamp, and the law a light, and reproofs of instruction are the way of life.

WISDOM 6:20–23

Hear, ye children, the instruction of a father, and attend, that you may know prudence. I will give you a good gift, forsake not my law. For I also was my father's son, tender, and as an only son in the sight of my mother: And he taught me, and said: Let thy heart receive my words, keep my commandments, and thou shalt live.

PROVERBS 4:1–4

The heart of the wise shall instruct his mouth: and shall add grace to his lips.

PROVERBS 16:23

Hear counsel, and receive instruction, that thou mayest be wise in thy latter end.

PROVERBS 19:20

Hear, O my son, and receive my words, that years of life may be multiplied to thee. I will shew thee the way of wisdom, I will lead thee by the paths of equity: Which when thou shalt have entered, thy steps shall not be straitened, and when thou runnest, thou shalt not meet a stumblingblock. Take hold on instruction, leave it not: keep it, because it is thy life.

PROVERBS 4:10–13

I charge you in the presence of God and of Christ Jesus, who will judge the living and the dead, and by his appearing and his kingly power: proclaim the word; be persistent whether it is convenient or inconvenient; convince, reprimand, encourage through all patience and teaching. For the time will come when people will not tolerate sound doctrine but, following their own desires and insatiable curiosity, will accumulate teachers and will stop listening to the truth and will be diverted to myths. But you, be self-possessed in all circumstances; put up with hardship; perform the work of an evangelist; fulfill your ministry.

2 TIMOTHY 4:1–5 NABRE

Continue thou in those things which thou hast learned and which have been committed to thee. Knowing of whom thou hast learned them: And because from thy infancy thou hast known the holy scriptures which can instruct thee to salvation by the faith which is in Christ Jesus. All scripture, inspired of God, is profitable to teach, to reprove, to correct, to instruct in justice: That the man of God may be perfect, furnished to every good work.

2 TIMOTHY 3:14–17

Jesus Christ
n.: The only begotten Son of God;
our Savior and Lord.

There shall come forth a rod out of the root of Jesse, and a flower shall rise up out of his root. And the spirit of the Lord shall rest upon him: the spirit of wisdom, and of understanding, the spirit of counsel, and of fortitude, the spirit of knowledge, and of godliness. And he shall be filled with the spirit of the fear of the Lord, He shall not judge according to the sight of the eyes, nor reprove according to the hearing of the ears. But he shall judge the poor with justice, and shall reprove with equity the meek of the earth: and he shall strike the earth with the rod of his mouth, and with the breath of his lips he shall slay the wicked.

Isaias 11:1–4

Jesus spoke to them, saying: I am the light of the world. He that followeth me walketh not in darkness, but shall have the light of life.

John 8:12

Therefore you have received Jesus Christ the Lord, walk ye in him: Rooted and built up in him and confirmed in the faith, as also you have learned: abounding in him in thanksgiving. Beware lest any man cheat you by philosophy and vain deceit: according to the tradition of men according to the elements of the world and not according to Christ. For in him dwelleth all the fulness of the Godhead corporeally. And you are filled in him, who is the head of all principality and power.

Colossians 2:6–10

Jesus Christ, yesterday, and today: and the same for ever.

Hebrews 13:8

Therefore if you be risen with Christ, seek the things that are above, where Christ is sitting at the right hand of God. Mind the things that are above, not the things that are upon the earth. For you are dead: and your life is hid with Christ in God. When Christ shall appear, who is your life, then you also shall appear with him in glory.

COLOSSIANS 3:1–4

The angel said to her: Fear not, Mary, for thou hast found grace with God. Behold thou shalt conceive in thy womb and shalt bring forth a son: and thou shalt call his name Jesus. He shall be great and shall be called the Son of the Most High. And the Lord God shall give unto him the throne of David his father: and he shall reign in the house of Jacob for ever. And of his kingdom there shall be no end.

LUKE 1:30–33

These things I write to you, that you may not sin. But if any man sin, we have an advocate with the Father, Jesus Christ the just. And he is the propitiation for our sins: and not for ours only, but also for those of the whole world.

1 JOHN 2:1–2

There is one God: and one mediator of God and men, the man Christ Jesus: Who gave himself a redemption for all, a testimony in due times.

1 TIMOTHY 2:5–6

Christ also died once for our sins, the just for the unjust: that he might offer us to God, being put to death indeed in the flesh, but enlivened in the spirit.

1 PETER 3:18

Joy

n.: A delight of the mind arising from the
consideration of a present or assured
possession of a future good.

They shall say in that day: Lo, this is our God, we have waited
for him, and he will save us: this is the Lord, we have patiently
waited for him, we shall rejoice and be joyful in his salvation.

ISAIAS 25:9

The fig tree shall not blossom: and there shall be no spring
in the vines. The labour of the olive tree shall fail: and the
fields shall yield no food: the flock shall be cut off from the
fold, and there shall be no herd in the stalls. But I will rejoice in the Lord: and I will joy in God my Jesus.

HABACUC 3:17–18

The redeemed of the Lord shall return, and shall come into
Sion with praise, and everlasting joy shall be upon their
heads: they shall obtain joy and gladness, and sorrow and
mourning shall flee away.

ISAIAS 35:10

They that are redeemed by the Lord, shall return, and shall
come into Sion singing praises, and joy everlasting shall be
upon their heads, they shall obtain joy and gladness, sorrow
and mourning shall flee away.

ISAIAS 51:11

You shall go out with joy, and be led forth with peace: the
mountains and the hills shall sing praise before you, and all
the trees of the country shall clap their hands. Instead of the
shrub, shall come up the fir tree, and instead of the nettle,
shall come up the myrtle tree: and the Lord shall be named
for an everlasting sign, that shall not be taken away.

ISAIAS 55:12–13

May those who sow in tears reap with shouts of joy! He that goes forth weeping, bearing the seed for sowing, shall come home with shouts of joy, bringing his sheaves with him.

PSALM 126:5–6

I foresaw the Lord before my face: because he is at my right hand, that I may not be moved. For this my heart hath been glad, and my tongue hath rejoiced: moreover my flesh also shall rest in hope. Because thou wilt not leave my soul in hell: nor suffer thy Holy One to see corruption. Thou hast made known to me the ways of life: thou shalt make me full of joy with thy countenance.

ACTS 2:25–28

Jesus Christ, whom having not seen, you love: in whom also now though you see him not, you believe and, believing, shall rejoice with joy unspeakable and glorified.

1 PETER 1:7–8

The God of hope fill you with all joy and peace in believing: that you may abound in hope and in the power of the Holy Ghost.

ROMANS 15:13

Blessed are ye that weep now: for you shall laugh. Blessed shall you be when men shall hate you, and when they shall separate you and shall reproach you and cast out your name as evil, for the Son of man's sake. Be glad in that day and rejoice: for behold, your reward is great in heaven, for according to these things did their fathers to the prophets.

LUKE 5:21–23

You now indeed have sorrow: but I will see you again and your heart shall rejoice. And your joy no man shall take from you.

JOHN 16:22

Kindness

n.: Zeal toward another in a good sense,
such as favors, benefits, or compassion.

For a small moment have I forsaken thee, but with great mercies will I gather thee. In a moment of indignation have I hid my face a little while from thee, but with everlasting kindness have I had mercy on thee, said the Lord thy Redeemer.

Isaias 54:7–8

Thus says the Lord: Let not the wise man glory in his wisdom, nor the strong man glory in his strength, nor the rich man glory in his riches; but rather, let him who glories, glory in this, that in his prudence he knows me, Knows that I, the Lord, bring about kindness, justice and uprightness on the earth; For with such am I pleased, says the Lord.

Jeremiah 9:22–23 nabre

Put on then, as God's chosen ones, holy and beloved, heartfelt compassion, kindness, humility, gentleness, and patience, bearing with one another and forgiving one another, if one has a grievance against another; as the Lord has forgiven you, so must you also do.

Colossians 3:12–13 nabre

All bitterness, fury, anger, shouting, and reviling must be removed from you, along with all malice. (And) be kind to one another, compassionate, forgiving one another as God has forgiven you in Christ.

Ephesians 4:31–32 nabre

Let not kindness and fidelity leave you; bind them around your neck; then will you win favor and good esteem before God and man.

PROVERBS 3:3–4 NABRE

The favors of the Lord I will recall, the glorious deeds of the Lord, Because of all he has done for us; for he is good to the house of Israel, He has favored us according to his mercy and his great kindness.

ISAIAH 63:7 NABRE

If God did not spare the natural branches, neither will he spare you. Note then the kindness and the severity of God: severity toward those who have fallen, but God's kindness to you, provided you continue in his kindness; otherwise you too will be cut off. And even the others, if they do not persist in their unbelief, will be grafted in, for God has the power to graft them in again. For if you have been cut from what is by nature a wild olive tree, and grafted, contrary to nature, into a cultivated olive tree, how much more will these natural branches be grafted back into their own olive tree.

ROMANS 11:21–24 RSV-CE

You have no excuse, O man, whoever you are, when you judge another; for in passing judgment upon him you condemn yourself, because you, the judge, are doing the very same things. We know that the judgment of God rightly falls upon those who do such things. Do you suppose, O man, that when you judge those who do such things and yet do them yourself, you will escape the judgment of God? Or do you presume upon the riches of his kindness and forbearance and patience? Do you not know that God's kindness is meant to lead you to repentance?

ROMANS 2:1–4 RSV-CE

Knowledge

*n.: The act of understanding and
having a clear perception of truth.*

Grace to you and peace be accomplished in the knowledge
of God and of Christ Jesus our Lord: As all things of his
divine power which appertain to life and godliness, are given
us, through the knowledge of him who hath called us by
his own proper glory and virtue. By whom he hath given us
most great and precious promises: that by these you may be
made partakers of the divine nature.

2 Peter 1:2–4

Grow in grace, and in the knowledge of our Lord and Saviour Jesus Christ. To him be glory both now and unto the
day of eternity. Amen.

2 Peter 3:18

Knowledge is a fountain of life to him that possesseth it: the
instruction of fools is foolishness. The heart of the wise shall
instruct his mouth: and shall add grace to his lips.

Proverbs 16:22–23

The fear of Yahweh is the beginning of knowledge; fools
spurn wisdom and discipline.

Proverbs 1:7 njb

You, employing all care, minister in your faith, virtue; and
in virtue, knowledge; and in knowledge, abstinence; and
in abstinence, patience; and in patience, godliness; and in
godliness, love of brotherhood; and in love of brotherhood,
charity. For if these things be with you and abound, they will
make you to be neither empty nor unfruitful in the knowledge of our Lord Jesus Christ.

2 Peter 1:5–8

We also, from the day that we heard it, cease not to pray for you, and to beg that you may be filled with the knowledge of his will, in all wisdom, and spiritual understanding: that you may walk worthy of God, in all things pleasing; being fruitful in every good work, and increasing in the knowledge of God.

COLOSSIANS 1:9–10

Thanks be to God, who always maketh us to triumph in Christ Jesus, and manifesteth the odor of his knowledge by us in every place. For we are the good odor of Christ unto God, in them that are saved, and in them that perish.

2 CORINTHIANS 2:14–15

This I pray, that your charity may more and more abound in knowledge, and in all understanding: That you may approve the better things, that you may be sincere and without offence unto the day of Christ, filled with the fruit of justice, through Jesus Christ, unto the glory and praise of God.

PHILIPPIANS 1:9–11

For God, who commanded the light to shine out of darkness, hath shined in our hearts, to give the light of the knowledge of the glory of God, in the face of Christ Jesus. But we have this treasure in earthen vessels, that the excellency may be of the power of God, and not of us.

2 CORINTHIANS 4:6–7

The simple acquire folly, but the prudent are crowned with knowledge.

PROVERBS 14:18 RSV-CE

There is gold, and a multitude of jewels: but the lips of knowledge are a precious vessel.

PROVERBS 20:15

Life

n.: The state of being a vital or functional being;
the sequence of physical, mental, or spiritual experiences
that make up the existence of an individual.

The grace of God our Saviour hath appeared to all men: instructing us, that, denying ungodliness and worldly desires, we should live soberly and justly and godly in this world, Looking for the blessed hope and coming of the glory of the great God and our Saviour Jesus Christ. Who gave himself for us, that he might redeem us from all iniquity and might cleanse to himself a people acceptable, a pursuer of good works.

Titus 2:10–14

Whoever lives an honest life will be safe, whoever wavers between two ways falls down in one of them.

Proverbs 28:18 njb

I call heaven and earth to witness this day, that I have set before you life and death, blessing and cursing. Choose therefore life, that both thou and thy seed may live: And that thou mayst love the Lord thy God, and obey his voice, and adhere to him (for he is thy life, and the length of thy days).

Deuteronomy 30:19–20

I shall utter words of wisdom from the heart, my lips will speak in all sincerity. God's was the spirit that made me, Shaddai's the breath that gave me life. Refute me, if you can.

Job 33:3–5 njb

Come, children, listen to me; I will teach you the fear of the Lord. Who among you loves life, takes delight in prosperous days? Keep your tongue from evil, your lips from speaking lies. Turn from evil and do good; seek peace and pursue it.

Psalm 34:12–15 nabre

If you be risen with Christ, seek the things that are above, where Christ is sitting at the right hand of God. Mind the things that are above, not the things that are upon the earth. For you are dead: and your life is hid with Christ in God. When Christ shall appear, who is your life, then you also shall appear with him in glory.

COLOSSIANS 3:1–4

The bread of God is that which cometh down from heaven and giveth life to the world. They said therefore unto him: Lord, give us always this bread. And Jesus said to them: I am the bread of life. He that cometh to me shall not hunger: and he that believeth in me shall never thirst.

JOHN 6:33–35

It is the spirit that gives life, while the flesh is of no avail. The words I have spoken to you are spirit and life.

JOHN 6:63 NABRE

The thief cometh not, but for to steal and to kill and to destroy. I am come that they may have life and may have it more abundantly. I am the good shepherd. The good shepherd giveth his life for his sheep.

JOHN 10:10–11

If Christ is in you, although your bodies are dead because of sin, your spirits are alive because of righteousness. If the Spirit of him who raised Jesus from the dead dwells in you, he who raised Christ Jesus from the dead will give life to your mortal bodies also through his Spirit which dwells in you.

ROMANS 8:10–11 RSV-CE

He who finds his life will lose it, and he who loses his life for my sake will find it.

MATTHEW 10:39 RSV-CE

Loneliness

n.: Sadness resulting from being alone,
without company.

The upright rejoice in the presence of God, delighted and crying out for joy. Sing to God, play music to his name, build a road for the Rider of the Clouds, rejoice in Yahweh, dance before him. Father of orphans, defender of widows, such is God in his holy dwelling. God gives the lonely a home to live in, leads prisoners out into prosperity.

PSALM 68:3–6 NJB

Let your manners be without covetousness, contented with such things as you have; for he hath said: I will not leave thee, neither will I forsake thee. So that we may confidently say: the Lord is my helper: I will not fear what man shall do to me.

HEBREWS 13:5–6

As in one body we have many members, but all the members have not the same office: So we being many, are one body in Christ, and every one members one of another.

ROMANS 12:4–5

Who then shall separate us from the love of Christ? Shall tribulation? or distress? or famine? or nakedness? or danger? or persecution? or the sword? (As it is written: For thy sake we are put to death all the day long. We are accounted as sheep for the slaughter.) But in all these things we overcome, because of him that hath loved us. For I am sure that neither death, nor life, nor angels, nor principalities, nor powers, nor things present, nor things to come, nor might, Nor height, nor depth, nor any other creature, shall be able to separate us from the love of God, which is in Christ Jesus our Lord.

ROMANS 8:35–39

I am always with you; you take hold of my right hand. With your counsel you guide me, and at the end receive me with honor. Whom else have I in the heavens? None beside you delights me on earth. Though my flesh and my heart fail, God is the rock of my heart, my portion forever.

Psalm 73:23–26 NABRE

I will ask the Father, and he shall give you another Paraclete, that he may abide with you for ever. The spirit of truth, whom the world cannot receive, because it seeth him not, nor knoweth him: but you shall know him; because he shall abide with you, and shall be in you. I will not leave you orphans, I will come to you. Yet a little while: and the world seeth me no more. But you see me: because I live, and you shall live. In that day you shall know, that I am in my Father, and you in me, and I in you.

John 14:16–20

Behold I am with you all days, even to the consummation of the world.

Matthew 28:20

I heard a loud voice call from the throne, "Look, here God lives among human beings. He will make his home among them; they will be his people, and he will be their God, God-with-them. He will wipe away all tears from their eyes; there will be no more death, and no more mourning or sadness or pain. The world of the past has gone."

Revelation 21:3–4 NJB

You are the temple of the living God; as God saith: I will dwell in them, and walk among them; and I will be their God, and they shall be my people.

2 Corinthians 6:16

Love

n.: Strong affection for another;
warm attachment or devotion.

What will separate us from the love of Christ? Will anguish, or distress, or persecution, or famine, or nakedness, or peril, or the sword? As it is written: "For your sake we are being slain all the day; we are looked upon as sheep to be slaughtered." No, in all these things we conquer overwhelmingly through him who loved us. For I am convinced that neither death, nor life, nor angels, nor principalities, nor present things, nor future things, nor powers, nor height, nor depth, nor any other creature will be able to separate us from the love of God in Christ Jesus our Lord.

ROMANS 8:35–39 NABRE

Put on then, as God's chosen ones, holy and beloved, heartfelt compassion, kindness, humility, gentleness, and patience, bearing with one another and forgiving one another, if one has a grievance against another; as the Lord has forgiven you, so must you also do. And over all these put on love, that is, the bond of perfection.

COLOSSIANS 3:12–14 NABRE

Though I command languages both human and angelic—if I speak without love, I am no more than a gong booming or a cymbal clashing. And though I have the power of prophecy, to penetrate all mysteries and knowledge, and though I have all the faith necessary to move mountains—if I am without love, I am nothing. Though I should give away to the poor all that I possess, and even give up my body to be burned—if I am without love, it will do me no good whatever.

1 CORINTHIANS 13:1–3 NJB

Love is always patient and kind; love is never jealous; love is not boastful or conceited, it is never rude and never seeks its own advantage, it does not take offence or store up grievances. Love does not rejoice at wrongdoing, but finds its joy in the truth. It is always ready to make allowances, to trust, to hope and to endure whatever comes. Love never comes to an end.

1 Corinthians 4:8 njb

I bow my knees before the Father, from whom every family in heaven and on earth is named, that according to the riches of his glory he may grant you to be strengthened with might through his Spirit in the inner man, and that Christ may dwell in your hearts through faith; that you, being rooted and grounded in love, may have power to comprehend with all the saints what is the breadth and length and height and depth, and to know the love of Christ which surpasses knowledge, that you may be filled with all the fulness of God.

Ephesians 3:14–19 rsv-ce

Be imitators of God, as beloved children. And walk in love, as Christ loved us and gave himself up for us, a fragrant offering and sacrifice to God.

Ephesians 5:1–2 rsv-ce

A new commandment I give unto you: That you love one another, as I have loved you, that you also love one another. By this shall all men know that you are my disciples, if you have love one for another.

John 13:34–35

He that hath my commandments and keepeth them; he it is that loveth me. And he that loveth me shall be loved of my Father: and I will love him and will manifest myself to him.

John 14:21

Marriage

n.: The state of being bound to another person
in a consensual and contractual relationship
recognized by law.

To avoid immorality every man should have his own wife
and every woman her own husband. The husband must give
to his wife what she has a right to expect, and so too the
wife to her husband. The wife does not have authority over
her own body, but the husband does; and in the same way,
the husband does not have authority over his own body, but
the wife does. You must not deprive each other, except by
mutual consent for a limited time, to leave yourselves free
for prayer, and to come together again afterwards; otherwise
Satan may take advantage of any lack of self-control to put
you to the test.

1 Corinthians 7:2–5 njb

Be subject to one another out of reverence for Christ. Wives
should be subject to their husbands as to the Lord, since,
as Christ is head of the Church and saves the whole body,
so is a husband the head of his wife; and as the Church is
subject to Christ, so should wives be to their husbands, in
everything.

Ephesians 5:21–24 njb

Husbands must love their wives as they love their own bodies; for a man to love his wife is for him to love himself. A
man never hates his own body, but he feeds it and looks after it; and that is the way Christ treats the Church, because
we are parts of his Body. This is why a man leaves his father
and mother and becomes attached to his wife, and the two
become one flesh.

Ephesians 5:28–31 njb

If one of the brothers has a wife who is not a believer, and she is willing to stay with him, he should not divorce her; and if a woman has a husband who is not a believer and he is willing to stay with her, she should not divorce her husband. You see, the unbelieving husband is sanctified through his wife and the unbelieving wife is sanctified through the brother. If this were not so, your children would be unclean, whereas in fact they are holy. But if the unbeliever chooses to leave, then let the separation take place: in these circumstances, the brother or sister is no longer tied. But God has called you to live in peace. Only, everyone should live as the Lord has assigned.

1 CORINTHIANS 7:12–15, 17 NJB

Let marriage be honored among all and the marriage bed be kept undefiled, for God will judge the immoral and adulterers.

HEBREWS 13:4 NABRE

An unmarried man is anxious about the things of the Lord, how he may please the Lord. But a married man is anxious about the things of the world, how he may please his wife, and he is divided. An unmarried woman or a virgin is anxious about the things of the Lord, so that she may be holy in both body and spirit. A married woman, on the other hand, is anxious about the things of the world, how she may please her husband. I am telling you this for your own benefit, not to impose a restraint upon you, but for the sake of propriety and adherence to the Lord without distraction.

1 CORINTHIANS 7:33–35 NABRE

Meditation

n.: The act or process of serious
contemplation or reflection.

Let not the book of this law depart from thy mouth: but thou shalt meditate on it day and night, that thou mayst observe and do all things that are written in it: then shalt thou direct thy way, and understand it.

JOSHUA 1:8

I remember the days of old, I meditate on all that thou hast done; I muse on what thy hands have wrought. I stretch out my hands to thee; my soul thirsts for thee like a parched land. [Selah] Make haste to answer me, O Lord! My spirit fails! Hide not thy face from me, lest I be like those who go down to the Pit. Let me hear in the morning of thy steadfast love, for in thee I put my trust. Teach me the way I should go, for to thee I lift up my soul.

PSALM 143:5–8 RSV-CE

I revere thy commandments, which I love, and I will meditate on thy statutes. Remember thy word to thy servant, in which thou hast made me hope. This is my comfort in my affliction that thy promise gives me life.

PSALM 119:48–50 RSV-CE

Blessed is the man who hath not walked in the counsel of the ungodly, nor stood in the way of sinners, nor sat in the chair of pestilence. But his will is in the law of the Lord, and on his law he shall meditate day and night. And he shall be like a tree which is planted near the running waters, which shall bring forth its fruit, in due season. And his leaf shall not fall off: and all whatsoever he shall do shall prosper.

PSALM 1:1–3

Oh, how I love thy law! It is my meditation all the day. Thy commandment makes me wiser than my enemies, for it is ever with me. I have more understanding than all my teachers, for thy testimonies are my meditation. I understand more than the aged, for I keep thy precepts. I hold back my feet from every evil way, in order to keep thy word. I do not turn aside from thy ordinances, for thou hast taught me. How sweet are thy words to my taste, sweeter than honey to my mouth!

PSALM 119:97–103 RSV-CE

Keep back thy servant also from presumptuous sins; let them not have dominion over me! Then I shall be blameless, and innocent of great transgression. Let the words of my mouth and the meditation of my heart be acceptable in thy sight, O Lord, my rock and my redeemer.

PSALM 19:13–14 RSV-CE

Blessed are you, Yahweh, teach me your will! With my lips I have repeated all the judgments you have given. In the way of your instructions lies my joy, a joy beyond all wealth. I will ponder your precepts and fix my gaze on your paths. I find my delight in your will, I do not forget your words.

PSALM 119:12–16 NJB

We reflect on your faithful love, God, in your temple! Both your name and your praise, God, are over the whole wide world. Your right hand is full of saving justice.

PSALM 48:9–10 NJB

On my bed when I think of you, I muse on you in the watches of the night, for you have always been my help; in the shadow of your wings I rejoice.

PSALM 63:6–7 NJB

Mercy

n.: Lenient or compassionate treatment
shown especially to an offender.

When the goodness and kindness of God our Saviour appeared: Not by the works of justice which we have done, but according to his mercy, he saved us, by the laver of regeneration and renovation of the Holy Ghost. Whom he hath poured forth upon us abundantly, through Jesus Christ our Saviour: that, being justified by his grace, we may be heirs according to hope of life everlasting.

TITUS 3:4–7

To the righteous a light is risen up in darkness: he is merciful, and compassionate and just. Acceptable is the man that sheweth mercy and lendeth: he shall order his words with judgment: Because he shall not be moved for ever.

PSALM 11:4–6

As you also in times past did not believe God, but now have obtained mercy, through their unbelief; so these also now have not believed, for your mercy, that they also may obtain mercy. For God hath concluded all in unbelief, that he may have mercy on all.

ROMANS 11:29–32

For a small moment have I forsaken thee, but with great mercies will I gather thee. For the mountains shall be moved, and the hills shall tremble; but my mercy shall not depart from thee, and the covenant of my peace shall not be moved: said the Lord that hath mercy on thee.

ISAIAS 54:7, 10

Yahweh is mercy and tenderness. He gives food to those who fear him, he keeps his covenant ever in mind.

PSALM 11:4–5 NJB

Look down from heaven and regard us from your holy and glorious palace! Where is your zealous care and your might, your surge of pity and your mercy? O Lord, hold not back, for you are our father.

ISAIAH 63:15–16 NABRE

I will shew thee, O man, what is good, and what the Lord requireth of thee: Verily, to do judgment, and to love mercy, and to walk solicitous with thy God.

MICHEAS 6:8

God, (who is rich in mercy,) for his exceeding charity wherewith he loved us, Even when we were dead in sins, hath quickened us together in Christ, (by whose grace you are saved,) and hath raised us up together, and hath made us sit together in the heavenly places, through Christ Jesus.

EPHESIANS 2:4–6

Speak ye, and so do, as being to be judged by the law of liberty. For judgment without mercy to him that hath not done mercy. And mercy exalteth itself above judgment.

JAMES 2:12–13

You, my beloved, building yourselves upon your most holy faith, praying in the Holy Ghost, keep yourselves in the love of God, waiting for the mercy of our Lord Jesus Christ, unto life everlasting.

JUDE 1:20–21

Miracles

n.: Extraordinary events believed to manifest
the supernatural work of God.

Give thanks to Yahweh, call his name aloud, proclaim his deeds
to the peoples. Chant to him, play to him, sing about all his
wonders! Take pride in his holy name, let your heart rejoice, you
seekers of Yahweh! Seek out Yahweh, seek his strength, continually seek out his presence! Remember what wonders he has
done, what miracles, what rulings he has given.

2 CHRONICLES 16:8–12 NJB

I said, "I am the Son of God? If I am not doing the works
of my Father, then do not believe me; but if I do them, even
though you do not believe me, believe the works, that you
may know and understand that the Father is in me and I am
in the Father."

JOHN 10:36–38 RSV-CE

A week later his disciples were again inside and Thomas
was with them. Jesus came, although the doors were locked,
and stood in their midst and said, "Peace be with you." Then
he said to Thomas, "Put your finger here and see my hands,
and bring your hand and put it into my side, and do not be
unbelieving, but believe." Thomas answered and said to him,
"My Lord and my God!" Jesus said to him, "Have you come
to believe because you have seen me? Blessed are those who
have not seen and have believed." Now Jesus did many other
signs in the presence of (his) disciples that are not written
in this book. But these are written that you may (come to)
believe that Jesus is the Messiah, the Son of God, and that
through this belief you may have life in his name.

JOHN 20:26–31 NABRE

Great is the Lord, and greatly to be praised, and his greatness is unsearchable. One generation shall laud thy works to another, and shall declare thy mighty acts. On the glorious splendor of thy majesty, and on thy wondrous works, I will meditate. Men shall proclaim the might of thy terrible acts, and I will declare thy greatness.

PSALM 145:3–6 RSV-CE

Wonderful things did he do in the sight of their fathers. . . . He divided the sea and brought them through: and he made the waters to stand as in a vessel. And he conducted them with a cloud by day: and all the night with a light of fire. He struck the rock in the wilderness: and gave them to drink, as out of the great deep. He brought forth water out of the rock: and made streams run down as rivers.

PSALM 77:11–16

As for me, I would seek God, and to God would I commit my cause; who does great things and unsearchable, marvelous things without number.

JOB 5:8–9 RSV-CE

There are diversities of operations, but the same God, who worketh all in all. And the manifestation of the Spirit is given to every man unto profit. To one indeed, by the Spirit, is given the word of wisdom: and to another, the word of knowledge, according to the same Spirit; to another, faith in the same spirit; to another, the grace of healing in one Spirit; to another, the working of miracles; to another, prophecy; to another, the discerning of spirits; to another, diverse kinds of tongues; to another, interpretation of speeches. But all these things one and the same Spirit worketh, dividing to every one according as he will.

1 CORINTHIANS 12:6–11

Obedience

*n.: The state or process of faithfully carrying out
the instructions and judgments of another.*

During his life on earth, he [Jesus] offered up prayer and
entreaty, with loud cries and with tears, to the one who had
the power to save him from death, and, winning a hearing
by his reverence, he learnt obedience, Son though he was,
through his sufferings; when he had been perfected, he became for all who obey him the source of eternal salvation.

HEBREWS 5:7–9 NJB

Sacrifice and offering you do not want; but ears open to
obedience you gave me. Holocausts and sin-offerings you do
not require; so I said, "Here I am; your commands for me are
written in the scroll. To do your will is my delight; my God,
your law is in my heart!"

PSALM 40:7–9 NABRE

When you hearken to the voice of the Lord, your God, all
these blessings will come upon you and overwhelm you:
"May you be blessed in the city, and blessed in the country!
Blessed be the fruit of your womb, the produce of your soil
and the offspring of your livestock, the issue of your herds
and the young of your flocks! Blessed be your grain bin and
your kneading bowl! May you be blessed in your coming in,
and blessed in your going out!"

DEUTERONOMY 28:2–6 NABRE

He opens their ears to correction and exhorts them to turn
back from evil. If they obey and serve him, they spend their
days in prosperity, their years in happiness. But if they obey
not, they perish; they die for lack of knowledge.

JOB 36:10–12 NABRE

Is Yahweh pleased by burnt offerings and sacrifices or by obedience to Yahweh's voice? Truly, obedience is better than sacrifice, submissiveness than the fat of rams.

1 Samuel 15:22 njb

If you keep my commandments, you will abide in my love, just as I have kept my Father's commandments and abide in his love. These things I have spoken to you, that my joy may be in you, and that your joy may be full.

John 15:10–11 rsv-ce

We know that we have come to know him, if we keep his commandments. Whoever says, "I know him" without keeping his commandments, is a liar, and truth has no place in him. But anyone who does keep his word, in such a one God's love truly reaches its perfection. This is the proof that we are in God.

1 John 2:3–5 njb

Whereas indeed he was the Son of God, he learned obedience by the things which he suffered: And being consummated, he became, to all that obey him, the cause of eternal salvation.

Hebrews 5:8–9

Know you not, that to whom you yield yourselves servants to obey, his servants you are whom you obey, whether it be of sin unto death, or of obedience unto justice. But thanks be to God, that you were the servants of sin, but have obeyed from the heart, unto that form of doctrine, into which you have been delivered. Being then freed from sin, we have been made servants of justice.

Romans 6:16–18

Patience

*n.: The capacity, habit, or fact of bearing pains
or trials calmly or without complaint; being kindly or tolerant;
not hasty or impetuous.*

Be patient therefore, brethren, until the coming of the Lord.
Behold, the husbandman waiteth for the precious fruit of
the earth: patiently bearing till he receive the early and latter rain. Be you therefore also patient, and strengthen your
hearts: for the coming of the Lord is at hand.

JAMES 5:7–8

Walk worthy of God, in all things pleasing; being fruitful in
every good work, and increasing in the knowledge of God:
strengthened with all might, according to the power of his
glory, in all patience and longsuffering with joy.

COLOSSIANS 1:10–11

Be patient therefore, brethren, until the coming of the Lord.
Behold, the husbandman waiteth for the precious fruit of
the earth: patiently bearing till he receive the early and latter rain. Be you therefore also patient, and strengthen your
hearts: for the coming of the Lord is at hand.

JAMES 5:7–8

We are saved by hope. But hope that is seen, is not hope. For
what a man seeth, why doth he hope for? But if we hope for
that which we see not, we wait for it with patience.

ROMANS 8:24–25

We beseech you, brethren, rebuke the unquiet, comfort the
feeble minded, support the weak, be patient towards all men.
See that none render evil for evil to any man; but ever follow
that which is good towards each other, and towards all men.

1 THESSALONIANS 5:14–15

Put ye on therefore, as the elect of God, holy, and beloved, the bowels of mercy, benignity, humility, modesty, patience: Bearing with one another, and forgiving one another, if any have a complaint against another: even as the Lord hath forgiven you, so do you also.

COLOSSIANS 3:12–13

A faithful saying, and worthy of all acceptation, that Christ Jesus came into this world to save sinners, of whom I am the chief. But for this cause have I obtained mercy: that in me first Christ Jesus might shew forth all patience, for the information of them that shall believe in him unto life everlasting.

1 TIMOTHY 1:15–16

The Lord delayeth not his promise, as some imagine, but dealeth patiently for your sake, not willing that any should perish, but that all should return to penance.

2 PETER 3:9

I waited patiently for the Lord; he inclined to me and heard my cry. He drew me up from the desolate pit, out of the miry bog, and set my feet upon a rock, making my steps secure. He put a new song in my mouth, a song of praise to our God. Many will see and fear, and put their trust in the Lord.

PSALM 40:1–3 RSV-CE

Be still before the Lord, and wait patiently for him; fret not yourself over him who prospers in his way, over the man who carries out evil devices!

PSALM 37:7 RSV-CE

Peace

n.: A state of tranquility or quiet.

Since we have been justified by faith, we have peace with God through our Lord Jesus Christ, through whom we have gained access (by faith) to this grace in which we stand, and we boast in hope of the glory of God.

ROMANS 5:1–2 NABRE

Let me hear what God the Lord will speak, for he will speak peace to his people, to his saints, to those who turn to him in their hearts. Surely his salvation is at hand for those who fear him, that glory may dwell in our land. Steadfast love and faithfulness will meet; righteousness and peace will kiss each other.

PSALM 85:8–10 RSV-CE

For the rest, brethren, rejoice, be perfect, take exhortation, be of one mind, have peace; and the God of peace and of love shall be with you.

2 CORINTHIANS 13:11

In Christ Jesus, you, who some time were afar off, are made nigh by the blood of Christ. For he is our peace, who hath made both one, and breaking down the middle wall of partition, the enmities in his flesh: making void the law of commandments contained in decrees; that he might make the two in himself into one new man, making peace; and might reconcile both to God in one body by the cross, killing the enmities in himself. And coming, he preached peace to you that were afar off, and peace to them that were nigh. For by him we have access both in one Spirit to the Father.

EPHESIANS 2:13–18

Where envying and contention is, there is inconstancy, and every evil work. But the wisdom, that is from above, first indeed is chaste, then peaceable, modest, easy to be persuaded, consenting to the good, full of mercy and good fruits, without judging, without dissimulation. And the fruit of justice is sown in peace, to them that make peace.

JAMES 3:16–18

Peace I leave with you, my peace I give unto you: not as the world giveth, do I give unto you. Let not your heart be troubled, nor let it be afraid.

JOHN 14:27

Have no anxiety at all, but in everything, by prayer and petition, with thanksgiving, make your requests known to God. Then the peace of God that surpasses all understanding will guard your hearts and minds in Christ Jesus. Finally, brothers, whatever is true, whatever is honorable, whatever is just, whatever is pure, whatever is lovely, whatever is gracious, if there is any excellence and if there is anything worthy of praise, think about these things. Keep on doing what you have learned and received and heard and seen in me. Then the God of peace will be with you.

PHILIPPIANS 4:6–9 NABRE

How then shall they call on him, in whom they have not believed? Or how shall they believe him, of whom they have not heard? And how shall they hear, without a preacher? And how shall they preach unless they be sent, as it is written: How beautiful are the feet of them that preach the gospel of peace, of them that bring glad tidings of good things!

ROMANS 10:14–15

Being justified therefore by faith, let us have peace with God, through our Lord Jesus Christ.

ROMANS 5:1

Persekution

*n.: The act of practice of harassing in
a manner to injure, grieve, or afflict.*

Blessed are they that suffer persecution for justice' sake: for
theirs is the kingdom of heaven. Blessed are ye when they
shall revile you, and persecute you, and speak all that is evil
against you, untruly, for my sake: Be glad and rejoice for
your reward is very great in heaven. For so they persecuted
the prophets that were before you.

Matthew 5:10–12

They will lay their hands upon you, and persecute you, de-
livering you up to the synagogues and into prisons, dragging
you before kings and governors, for my name's sake. And it
shall happen unto you for a testimony. Lay it up therefore
into your hearts, not to meditate before how you shall answer: for I will give you a mouth and wisdom, which all your
adversaries shall not be able to resist and gainsay.

Luke 21:12–15

We are reviled, and we bless; we are persecuted, and we suffer
it. We are blasphemed, and we entreat; we are made as the
refuse of this world, the offscouring of all even until now. . . .
Wherefore I beseech you, be ye followers of me, as I also am
of Christ.

1 Corinthians 4:12–13, 16

In all things we suffer tribulation, but are not distressed; we
are straitened, but are not destitute; We suffer persecution, but
are not forsaken; we are cast down, but we perish not: Always
bearing about in our body the mortification of Jesus, that the
life also of Jesus may be made manifest in our bodies.

2 Corinthians 4:8–10

Thou hast fully known my doctrine, manner of life, purpose, faith, longsuffering, love, patience, Persecutions, afflictions: such as came upon me at Antioch, at Iconium and at Lystra: what persecutions I endured, and out of them all the Lord delivered me. And all that will live godly in Christ Jesus shall suffer persecution.

2 Timothy 3:10–12

You have heard how it was said, You will love your neighbour and hate your enemy. But I say this to you, love your enemies and pray for those who persecute you; so that you may be children of your Father in heaven, for he causes his sun to rise on the bad as well as the good, and sends down rain to fall on the upright and the wicked alike.

Matthew 5:43–45 njb

If the world hate you, know ye, that it hath hated me before you. If you had been of the world, the world would love its own: but because you are not of the world, but I have chosen you out of the world, therefore the world hateth you. Remember my word that I said to you: The servant is not greater than his master. If they have persecuted me, they will also persecute you: if they have kept my word, they will keep yours also.

John 15:18–20

Who then shall separate us from the love of Christ? Shall tribulation? or distress? or famine? or nakedness? or danger? or persecution? or the sword? (As it is written: For thy sake we are put to death all the day long. We are accounted as sheep for the slaughter.) But in all these things we overcome, because of him that hath loved us.

Romans 8:35–37

Prayer

n.: The act of addressing God, whether in the form of entreaty, supplication, adoration, confession, or thanksgiving.

They will not toil in vain, nor bear children destined to disaster, for they are the race of Yahweh's blessed ones and so are their offspring. Thus, before they call I shall answer, before they stop speaking I shall have heard.

Isaias 65:23–24 njb

I have labored in my groanings, every night I will wash my bed: I will water my couch with my tears. My eye is troubled through indignation: I have grown old amongst all my enemies. Depart from me, all ye workers of iniquity: for the Lord hath heard the voice of my weeping. The Lord hath heard my supplication: the Lord hath received my prayer.

Psalm 6:6–10

This is the confidence which we have towards him: That, whatsoever we shall ask according to his will, he heareth us. And we know that he heareth us whatsoever we ask: we know that we have the petitions which we request of him.

John 5:14–15

Say unto you, all things, whatsoever you ask when ye pray, believe that you shall receive; and they shall come unto you. And when you shall stand to pray, forgive, if you have aught against any man; that your Father also, who is in heaven, may forgive you your sins.

Mark 11:24–25

Give ear, O Lord, to my words, understand my cry. Hearken to the voice of my prayer, O my King and my God. For to thee will I pray: O Lord, in the morning thou shalt hear my voice.

PSALM 5:1–2

When thou shalt pray, enter into thy chamber, and having shut the door, pray to thy Father in secret: and thy Father who seeth in secret will repay thee. And when you are praying, speak not much, as the heathens. For they think that in their much speaking they may be heard. Be not you therefore like to them, for your Father knoweth what is needful for you, before you ask him.

MATTHEW 6:6–8

One of his disciples said to him, "Lord, teach us to pray just as John taught his disciples." He said to them, "When you pray, say: Father, hallowed be your name, your kingdom come. Give us each day our daily bread and forgive us our sins for we ourselves forgive everyone in debt to us, and do not subject us to the final test."

LUKE 11:1–4 NABRE

The Spirit also helpeth our infirmity. For we know not what we should pray for as we ought; but the Spirit himself asketh for us with unspeakable groanings. And he that searcheth the hearts, knoweth what the Spirit desireth; because he asketh for the saints according to God.

ROMANS 8:26–27

I desire therefore, first of all, that supplications, prayers, intercessions, and thanksgivings be made for all men: For kings, and for all that are in high station: that we may lead a quiet and a peaceable life in all piety and chastity. For this is good and acceptable in the sight of God our Saviour.

1 TIMOTHY 2:1–2

Protection

*n.: The state of being covered or shielded
from injury or destruction.*

You have the Lord for your refuge; you have made the Most
High your stronghold. No evil shall befall you, no affliction
come near your tent. For God commands the angels to
guard you in all your ways. With their hands they shall
support you, lest you strike your foot against a stone. You
shall tread upon the asp and the viper, trample the lion and
the dragon. Whoever clings to me I will deliver; whoever
knows my name I will set on high. All who call upon me
I will answer; I will be with them in distress; I will deliver
them and give them honor.

PSALM 91:9–15 NABRE

Though I walk in the midst of dangers, you guard my life
when my enemies rage. You stretch out your hand; your
right hand saves me. The Lord is with me to the end. Lord,
your love endures forever. Never forsake the work of your
hands!

PSALM 139:7–8 NABRE

I announced your deed to a great assembly; I did not restrain
my lips; you, Lord, are my witness. Your deed I did not hide
within my heart; your loyal deliverance I have proclaimed.
I made no secret of your enduring kindness to a great
assembly. Lord, do not withhold your compassion from me;
may your enduring kindness ever preserve me. For all about
me are evils beyond count; my sins so overcome me I cannot
see. They are more than the hairs of my head; my courage
fails me. Lord, graciously rescue me! Come quickly to help
me, Lord!

PSALM 40:10–14 NABRE

He [the Lord] will keep the salvation of the righteous, and protect them that walk in simplicity. Keeping the paths of justice, and guarding the ways of saints.

PROVERBS 2:7–8

The Lord is my helper and my protector: in him hath my heart confided, and I have been helped. And my flesh hath flourished again, and with my will I will give praise to him. The Lord is the strength of his people, and the protector of the salvation of his anointed.

PSALM 27:7–8

No weapon that is formed against thee shall prosper: and every tongue that resisteth thee in judgment, thou shalt condemn. This is the inheritance of the servants of the Lord, and their justice with me, saith the Lord.

ISAIAS 54:17

Brethren, pray for us, that the word of God may run, and may be glorified, even as among you; And that we may be delivered from importunate and evil men; for all men have not faith. But God is faithful, who will strengthen and keep you from evil.

2 THESSALONIANS 3:1–2

He [God] hath said: I will not leave thee, neither will I forsake thee. So that we may confidently say: The Lord is my helper: I will not fear what man shall do to me.

HEBREWS 13:5–6

He is my God and my savior: he is my protector, I shall be moved no more. Be thou, O my soul, subject to God: for from him is my patience. For he is my God and my savior: he is my helper, I shall not be moved.

PSALM 61:3, 6–7

Provision

n.: Necessary goods or supply.

I have all that I need and more: I am fully provided, now
that I have received from Epaphroditus the offering that you
sent, a pleasing smell, the sacrifice which is acceptable and
pleasing to God. And my God will fulfil all your needs out
of the riches of his glory in Christ Jesus. And so glory be to
God our Father, for ever and ever. Amen.

PHILIPPIANS 4:18–20 NJB

You won renown for your wondrous deeds; gracious and
merciful is the Lord. You gave food to those who fear you,
mindful of your covenant forever.

PSALM 11:4–5 NABRE

We also are mortals, men like unto you, preaching to you to
be converted from these vain things, to the living God, who
made the heaven, and the earth, and the sea, and all things
that are in them: Who in times past suffered all nations to
walk in their own ways. Nevertheless he left not himself
without testimony, doing good from heaven, giving rains and
fruitful seasons, filling our hearts with food and gladness.

ACTS 14:14–16

God is able to make all grace abound in you; that ye always,
having all sufficiency in all things, may abound to every
good work, As it is written: He hath dispersed abroad, he
hath given to the poor: his justice remaineth for ever. And
he that ministereth seed to the sower, will both give you
bread to eat, and will multiply your seed, and increase the
growth of the fruits of your justice: That being enriched in
all things, you may abound unto all simplicity, which worketh through us thanksgiving to God.

2 CORINTHIANS 9:8–11

Behold this day I am going into the way of all the earth, and you shall know with all your mind that of all the words which the Lord promised to perform for you, not one hath failed. Therefore as he hath fulfilled in deed, what he promised, and all things prosperous have come.

JOSHUA 23:14–15

Neither in my youth, nor now in old age have I ever seen the just abandoned or their children begging bread. The just always lend generously, and their children become a blessing.

PSALM 37:25–26 NABRE

I say to you, be not solicitous for your life, what you shall eat, nor for your body, what you shall put on. Is not the life more than the meat: and the body more than the raiment? Behold the birds of the air, for they neither sow, nor do they reap, nor gather into barns: and your heavenly Father feedeth them. Are not you of much more value than they?

MATTHEW 6:24–26

For raiment why are you solicitous? Consider the lilies of the field, how they grow: they labour not, neither do they spin. But I say to you, that not even Solomon in all his glory was arrayed as one of these. And if the grass of the field, which is today, and tomorrow is cast into the oven, God doth so clothe: how much more you, O ye of little faith? Be not solicitous therefore, saying, What shall we eat: or what shall we drink, or wherewith shall we be clothed? For after all these things do the heathens seek. For your Father knoweth that you have need of all these things.

MATTHEW 6:28–32

Purity

n.: The state of being untainted;
not mixed with anything else.

The temple of God cannot compromise with false gods, and that is what we are—the temple of the living God. We have God's word for it: I shall fix my home among them and live among them; I will be their God and they will be my people. Get away from them, purify yourselves, says the Lord. Do not touch anything unclean, and then I shall welcome you. I shall be father to you, and you will be sons and daughters to me, says the almighty Lord.

2 Corinthians 6:16–18 njb

Who may go up the mountain of the Lord? Who can stand in his holy place? The clean of hand and pure of heart, who are not devoted to idols, who have not sworn falsely. They will receive blessings from the Lord, and justice from their saving God.

Psalm 24:3–5 nabre

Beloved, we are God's children now; it does not yet appear what we shall be, but we know that when he appears we shall be like him, for we shall see him as he is. And every one who thus hopes in him purifies himself as he is pure.

1 John 3:2–3 rsv-ce

Drive out a scoffer, and strife will go out, and quarreling and abuse will cease. He who loves purity of heart, and whose speech is gracious, will have the king as his friend.

Proverbs 22:10–11 rsv-ce

If we say that we share in God's life while we are living in darkness, we are lying, because we are not living the truth. But if we live in light, as he is in light, we have a share in another's life, and the blood of Jesus, his Son, cleanses us from all sin.

1 JOHN 1:6–7

Blessed are those whose way is blameless, who walk in the law of the Lord! Blessed are those who keep his testimonies, who seek him with their whole heart, who also do no wrong, but walk in his ways!

PSALM 119:1–3 RSV-CE

Blessed are they that hunger and thirst after justice: for they shall have their fill. Blessed are the merciful: for they shall obtain mercy. Blessed are the clean of heart: for they shall see God. Blessed are the peacemakers: for they shall be called children of God.

MATTHEW 5:6–9

Draw nigh to God, and he will draw nigh to you. Cleanse your hands, ye sinners: and purify your hearts, ye double minded. Be afflicted, and mourn, and weep: let your laughter be turned into mourning, and your joy into sorrow. Be humbled in the sight of the Lord, and he will exalt you.

JAMES 4:8–10

I will praise thee with an upright heart, when I learn thy righteous ordinances. I will observe thy statutes; O forsake me not utterly! How can a young man keep his way pure? By guarding it according to thy word.

PSALM 119:7–9 RSV-CE

Purpose

n.: Something set up as an end
to be obtained; an intention.

We know that all things work for good for those who love God, who are called according to his purpose.

ROMANS 8:28 NABRE

When God wanted to give the heirs of his promise an even clearer demonstration of the immutability of his purpose, he intervened with an oath, so that by two immutable things, in which it was impossible for God to lie, we who have taken refuge might be strongly encouraged to hold fast to the hope that lies before us. This we have as an anchor of the soul, sure and firm.

HEBREWS 6:17–19 NABRE

In [Christ] whom we also are called by lot, being predestinated according to the purpose of him who worketh all things according to the counsel of his will. That we may be unto the praise of his glory: we who before hoped in Christ.

EPHESIANS 1:11–12 RSV-CE

[God] has saved us and called us to be holy—not because of anything we ourselves had done but for his own purpose and by his own grace. This grace had already been granted to us, in Christ Jesus, before the beginning of time.

2 TIMOTHY 1:9 NJB

We always pray for you, that our God may make you worthy of his calling and powerfully bring to fulfillment every good purpose and every effort of faith, that the name of our Lord Jesus may be glorified in you, and you in him, in accord with the grace of our God and Lord Jesus Christ.

2 THESSALONIANS 1:11–12 NABRE

Grace be to you, and peace from God the Father, and from the Lord Jesus Christ. Blessed be the God and Father of our Lord Jesus Christ, who hath blessed us with spiritual blessings in heavenly places, in Christ: As he chose us in him before the foundation of the world, that we should be holy and unspotted in his sight in charity. Who hath predestinated us unto the adoption of children through Jesus Christ unto himself: according to the purpose of his will.

EPHESIANS 1:2–5

Unto the praise of the glory of his grace, in which he hath graced us in his beloved son. In whom we have redemption through his blood, the remission of sins, according to the riches of his grace, which hath superabounded in us in all wisdom and prudence, that he might make known unto us the mystery of his will, according to his good pleasure, which he hath purposed in him, in the dispensation of the fulness of times, to re-establish all things in Christ, that are in heaven and on earth, in him.

EPHESIANS 1:6–10

Though I walk in the midst of trouble, thou dost preserve my life; thou dost stretch out thy hand against the wrath of my enemies, and thy right hand delivers me. The Lord will fulfil his purpose for me; thy steadfast love, O Lord, endures for ever. Do not forsake the work of thy hands.

PSALM 138:7–8 RSV-CE

Therefore, my beloved, as you have always obeyed, so now, not only as in my presence but much more in my absence, work out your own salvation with fear and trembling; for God is at work in you, both to will and to work for his good pleasure.

PHILIPPIANS 2:12–13 RSV-CE

Quietness & Solitude

*n.: A state marked by little or no activity, sounds,
or distractions; tranquility; aloneness.*

I desire therefore, first of all, that supplications, prayers, intercessions and thanksgivings be made for all men: For kings and
for all that are in high station: that we may lead a quiet and
a peaceable life in all piety and chastity. For this is good and
acceptable in the sight of God our Savior.

1 TIMOTHY 2:1–3

Then will the desert become an orchard and the orchard be
regarded as a forest. Right will dwell in the desert and justice abide in the orchard. Justice will bring about peace; right
will produce calm and security. My people will live in peaceful country, in secure dwellings and quiet resting places.

ISAIAH 32:15–18 NABRE

The Lord is my portion, said my soul: therefore will I wait
for him. The Lord is good to them that hope in him, to the
soul that seeketh him. It is good to wait with silence for the
salvation of God.

LAMENTATIONS 3:24–26

Be still, and know that I am God. I am exalted among the
nations, I am exalted in the earth! The Lord of hosts is with us.

PSALM 46:10–11 RSV-CE

Lord, my heart is not proud; nor are my eyes haughty. I do
not busy myself with great matters, with things too sublime
for me. Rather, I have stilled my soul, hushed it like a weaned
child. Like a weaned child on its mother's lap, so is my soul
within me. Israel, hope in the Lord, now and forever.

PSALM 131:1–3 NABRE

We entreat you, brethren, that you abound more: and that you use your endeavor to be quiet, and that you do your own business, and work with your own hands, as we commanded you: and that you walk honestly towards them that are without; and that you want nothing of any man's.

1 THESSALONIANS 4:10–11

I desire therefore, first of all, that supplications, prayers, intercessions, and thanksgivings be made for all men: For kings, and for all that are in high station: that we may lead a quiet and a peaceable life in all piety and chastity. For this is good and acceptable in the sight of God our Saviour, Who will have all men to be saved, and to come to the knowledge of the truth.

1 TIMOTHY 2:1–4

I said that wisdom is better than strength: how then is the wisdom of the poor man slighted, and his words not heard? The words of the wise are heard in silence, more than the cry of a prince among fools.

ECCLESIASTES 9:16–17

The Lord thy God in the midst of thee is mighty, he will save: he will rejoice over thee with gladness, he will be silent in his love, he will be joyful over thee in praise.

ZEPHANIAH 3:17

Thus saith the Lord God the Holy One of Israel: If you return and be quiet, you shall be saved: in silence and in hope shall your strength be.

ISAIAS 30:15

Reconciliation

n.: The act or process of restoring relationship with someone.

Anyone who is in Christ, there is a new creation: the old order is gone and a new being is there to see. It is all God's work; he reconciled us to himself through Christ and he gave us the ministry of reconciliation. I mean, God was in Christ reconciling the world to himself, not holding any-one's faults against them, but entrusting to us the message of reconciliation. So we are ambassadors for Christ; it is as though God were urging you through us, and in the name of Christ we appeal to you to be reconciled to God.

2 CORINTHIANS 5:17–20 NJB

In him [Jesus], it hath well pleased the Father, that all full-ness should dwell; and through him to reconcile all things unto himself, making peace through the blood of his cross, both as to the things that are on earth, and the things that are in heaven. And you, whereas you were some time alien-ated and enemies in mind in evil works: yet now he hath reconciled in the body of his flesh through death, to present you holy and unspotted, and blameless before him.

COLOSSIANS 1:19–22

I tell you, all that you ask for in prayer, believe that you will receive it and it shall be yours. When you shall stand to pray, forgive, if you have aught against any man; that your Father also, who is in heaven, may forgive you your sins. But if you will not forgive, neither will your Father that is in heaven, forgive you your sins.

MARK 11:24–26 NABRE

God commendeth his charity towards us; because when as yet we were sinners, according to the time, Christ died for us; much more therefore, being now justified by his blood, shall we be saved from wrath through him. For if, when we were enemies, we were reconciled to God by the death of his Son; much more, being reconciled, shall we be saved by his life. And not only so; but also we glory in God, through our Lord Jesus Christ, by whom we have now received reconciliation.

ROMANS 5:8–11

In Christ Jesus, you, who some time were afar off, are made nigh by the blood of Christ. For he is our peace, who hath made both one, and breaking down the middle wall of partition, the enmities in his flesh: making void the law of commandments contained in decrees; that he might make the two in himself into one new man, making peace; and might reconcile both to God in one body by the cross, killing the enmities in himself. And coming, he preached peace to you that were afar off, and peace to them that were nigh. For by him we have access both in one Spirit to the Father.

EPHESIANS 2:13–18

If therefore thou offer thy gift at the altar, and there thou remember that thy brother hath any thing against thee; leave there thy offering before the altar, and go first to be reconciled to thy brother: and then coming thou shalt offer thy gift.

MATTHEW 5:23–24

Why do you not judge for yourselves what is right? If you are to go with your opponent before a magistrate, make an effort to settle the matter on the way.

LUKE 12:58 NABRE

Redemption

n.: The act or process of buying or winning back; repurchasing.

I have blotted out thy iniquities as a cloud, and thy sins as a mist: return to me, for I have redeemed thee. Give praise, O ye heavens, for the Lord hath shewn mercy: shout with joy, ye ends of the earth: ye mountains, resound with praise, thou, O forest, and every tree therein.

ISAIAS 44:22–23

I called upon your name, O Lord, from the bottom of the pit; You heard me call, "Let not your ear be deaf to my cry for help!" You came to my aid when I called to you; you said, "Have no fear!" You defended me in mortal danger, you redeemed my life.

LAMENTATIONS 3:55–58 NABRE

Giving thanks to God the Father, who hath made us worthy to be partakers of the lot of the saints in light: who hath delivered us from the power of darkness, and hath translated us into the kingdom of the Son of his love, in whom we have redemption through his blood, the remission of sins.

COLOSSIANS 1:12–14

You were not redeemed with corruptible things as gold or silver, from your vain conversation of the tradition of your fathers: but with the precious blood of Christ, as of a lamb unspotted and undefiled, foreknown indeed before the foundation of the world, but manifested in the last times for you.

1 PETER 1:18–20

Hope in the Lord! For with the Lord there is steadfast love, and with him is plenteous redemption.

PSALM 130:7 RSV-CE

Neither by the blood of goats, or of calves, but by his own blood, entered once into the holies, having obtained eternal redemption. For if the blood of goats and of oxen, and the ashes of an heifer being sprinkled, sanctify such as are defiled, to the cleansing of the flesh: how much more shall the blood of Christ, who by the Holy Ghost offered himself unspotted unto God, cleanse our conscience from dead works, to serve the living God? And therefore he is the mediator of the new testament: that by means of his death, for the redemption of those transgressions, which were under the former testament, they that are called may receive the promise of eternal inheritance.

HEBREWS 9:12–15

All have sinned, and do need the glory of God. Being justified freely by his grace, through the redemption, that is in Christ Jesus, whom God hath proposed to be a propitiation, through faith in his blood, to the shewing of his justice, for the remission of former sins.

ROMANS 3:23–25

Christ hath redeemed us from the curse of the law, being made a curse for us: for it is written: Cursed is every one that hangeth on a tree: that the blessing of Abraham might come on the Gentiles through Christ Jesus: that we may receive the promise of the Spirit by faith.

GALATIANS 3:13–14

Relationships

n.: The state or process of being mutually or reciprocally connected with another person.

Consider, brothers, how you were called; not many of you are wise by human standards, not many influential, not many from noble families. No, God chose those who by human standards are fools to shame the wise; he chose those who by human standards are weak to shame the strong, those who by human standards are common and contemptible—indeed those who count for nothing—to reduce to nothing all those that do count for something, so that no human being might feel boastful before God. It is by him that you exist in Christ Jesus, who for us was made wisdom from God, and saving justice and holiness and redemption. As scripture says: If anyone wants to boast, let him boast of the Lord.

1 CORINTHIANS 1:26–31 NJB

I therefore, a prisoner in the Lord, beseech you that you walk worthy of the vocation in which you are called, with all humility and mildness, with patience, supporting one another in charity. Careful to keep the unity of the Spirit in the bond of peace.

EPHESIANS 4:1–2

We beseech you, brethren, to know them who labour among you, and are over you in the Lord, and admonish you: That you esteem them more abundantly in charity, for their work's sake. Have peace with them. And we beseech you, brethren, rebuke the unquiet, comfort the feeble minded, support the weak, be patient towards all men. See that none render evil for evil to any man; but ever follow that which is good towards each other, and towards all men.

1 THESSALONIANS 5:12–15

Do not be mismated with unbelievers. For what partnership have righteousness and iniquity? Or what fellowship has light with darkness? What accord has Christ with Be'lial? Or what has a believer in common with an unbeliever? What agreement has the temple of God with idols? For we are the temple of the living God; as God said, "I will live in them and move among them, and I will be their God, and they shall be my people. Therefore come out from them, and be separate from them," says the Lord, "and touch nothing unclean; then I will welcome you, and I will be a father to you, and you shall be my sons and daughters," says the Lord Almighty.

2 Corinthians 6:14–18 rsv-ce

Let all bitterness, and anger, and indignation, and clamour, and blasphemy, be put away from you, with all malice. And be ye kind one to another; merciful, forgiving one another, even as God hath forgiven you in Christ.

Ephesians 4:31–32

Bear ye one another's burdens; and so you shall fulfill the law of Christ. For if any man think himself to be some thing, whereas he is nothing, he deceiveth himself. But let every one prove his own work, and so he shall have glory in himself only, and not in another. For every one shall bear his own burden.

Galatians 6:2–5

If we walk in the light, as he also is in the light, we have fellowship one with another, and the blood of Jesus Christ his Son cleanseth us from all sin.

1 John 1:7

Repentance

n.: The act or process of turning from sin and determining to do what is right, especially in regard to misdeeds or moral shortcomings.

There is one thing, my dear friends, that you must never forget: that with the Lord, a day is like a thousand years, and a thousand years are like a day. The Lord is not being slow in carrying out his promises, as some people think he is; rather is he being patient with you, wanting nobody to be lost and everybody to be brought to repentance.

2 Peter 3:8–9 njb

I know, brothers, that neither you nor your leaders had any idea what you were really doing; but this was the way God carried out what he had foretold, when he said through all his prophets that his Christ would suffer. Now you must repent and turn to God, so that your sins may be wiped out, and so that the Lord may send the time of comfort. Then he will send you the Christ he has predestined, that is Jesus.

Acts 3:17–20 njb

Seek ye the Lord, while he may be found: call upon him, while he is near. Let the wicked forsake his way, and the unjust man his thoughts, and let him return to the Lord, and he will have mercy on him, and to our God: for he is bountiful to forgive.

Isaias 55:6–7

When the wicked turneth himself away from his wickedness, which he hath wrought, and doeth judgment, and justice: he shall save his soul alive. Because he considereth and turneth away himself from all his iniquities which he hath wrought, he shall surely live, and not die.

Ezekiel 18:27–28

Hearing this, they were cut to the heart and said to Peter and the other apostles, "What are we to do, brothers?" "You must repent," Peter answered, "and every one of you must be baptized in the name of Jesus Christ for the forgiveness of your sins, and you will receive the gift of the Holy Spirit. The promise that was made is for you and your children, and for all those who are far away, for all those whom the Lord our God is calling to himself."

ACTS 2:37–39 NJB

The tax collectors and sinners were all drawing near to listen to him, but the Pharisees and scribes began to complain, saying, "This man welcomes sinners and eats with them." So to them he addressed this parable. "What man among you having a hundred sheep and losing one of them would not leave the ninety-nine in the desert and go after the lost one until he finds it? And when he does find it, he sets it on his shoulders with great joy and, upon his arrival home, he calls together his friends and neighbors and says to them, 'Rejoice with me because I have found my lost sheep.' I tell you, in just the same way there will be more joy in heaven over one sinner who repents than over ninety-nine righteous people who have no need of repentance."

LUKE 15:1–7 NABRE

I rejoice, not because you were grieved, but because you were grieved into repenting; for you felt a godly grief, so that you suffered no loss through us. For godly grief produces a repentance that leads to salvation and brings no regret, but worldly grief produces death.

2 CORINTHIANS 7:9–10 RSV-CE

Respect

*n.: An act or attitude of giving high regard
to something or someone; honor.*

Therefore one must be subject, not only to avoid God's wrath but also for the sake of conscience. For the same reason you also pay taxes, for the authorities are ministers of God, attending to this very thing. Pay all of them their dues, taxes to whom taxes are due, revenue to whom revenue is due, respect to whom respect is due, honor to whom honor is due.

ROMANS 13:5–7 RSV-CE

For this reason a man shall leave his father and mother and be joined to his wife, and the two shall become one flesh. This mystery is a profound one, and I am saying that it refers to Christ and the church; however, let each one of you love his wife as himself, and let the wife see that she respects her husband.

EPHESIANS 5:31–33 RSV-CE

Aspire to live quietly, to mind your own affairs, and to work with your hands, as we charged you; so that you may command the respect of outsiders.

1 THESSALONIANS 4:11–12 RSV-CE

We beseech you, brethren, to respect those who labor among you and are over you in the Lord and admonish you, and to esteem them very highly in love because of their work. Be at peace among yourselves.

1 THESSALONIANS 5:12–13 RSV-CE

Live as servants of God. Honor all men. Love the brotherhood. Fear God. Honor the emperor. Servants, be submissive to your masters with all respect, not only to the kind
and gentle but also to the overbearing. For one is approved
if, mindful of God, he endures pain while suffering unjustly.

1 Peter 2:16–19 RSV-CE

We have had earthly fathers to discipline us and we
respected them. Shall we not much more be subject to the
Father of spirits and live? For they disciplined us for a short
time at their pleasure, but he disciplines us for our good,
that we may share his holiness.

Hebrews 12:9–10 RSV-CE

Contempt for the word is self-destructive, respect for the
commandment wins salvation. The teaching of the wise is a
life-giving fountain for eluding the snares of death.

Proverbs 13:13–14 NJB

The just man, if he be prevented with death, shall be in rest.
For his soul pleased God: therefore he hastened to bring
him out of the midst of iniquities: but the people see this,
and understand not, nor lay up such things in their hearts:
that the grace of God, and his mercy is with his saints, and
that he hath respect to his chosen.

Wisdom 4:7, 14–15

Long life comes to anyone who honors a father, whoever
obeys the Lord makes a mother happy. Such a one serves
parents as well as the Lord. Respect your father in deed as
well as word, so that blessing may come on you from him;
since a father's blessing makes his children's house firm.

Sirach 3:6–9 NJB

Rest

*n.: A state characterized by minimal functional
and metabolic activity; freedom from activity;
restorative inactivity.*

Come to me, all who labor and are heavy laden, and I will
give you rest. Take my yoke upon you, and learn from me;
for I am gentle and lowly in heart, and you will find rest for
your souls. For my yoke is easy, and my burden is light.

MATTHEW 11:28–30 RSV-CE

There remaineth therefore a day of rest for the people of
God. For he that is entered into his rest, the same also hath
rested from his works, as God did from his. Let us hasten
therefore to enter into that rest.

HEBREWS 4:9–11

The Lord will give thee rest continually, and will fill thy soul
with brightness, and deliver thy bones, and thou shalt be like
a watered garden, and like a fountain of water whose waters
shall not fail.

ISAIAS 58:11

If thou sleep, thou shalt not fear: thou shalt rest, and thy
sleep shall be sweet. Be not afraid of sudden fear, nor of the
power of the wicked falling upon thee. For the Lord will be
at thy side, and will keep thy foot that thou be not taken.

PROVERBS 3:24–26

Gracious is the Lord and just; yes, our God is merciful. The
Lord protects the simple; I was helpless, but God saved me.
Return, my soul, to your rest; the Lord has been good to you.
For my soul has been freed from death, my eyes from tears,
my feet from stumbling.

PSALM 116:5–8 NABRE

My soul rests in God alone, from whom comes my salvation. God alone is my rock and salvation, my secure height; I
shall never fall. My soul, be at rest in God alone, from whom
comes my hope. God alone is my rock and my salvation, my
secure height; I shall not fall. My safety and glory are with
God, my strong rock and refuge.

PSALM 62:2–3, 6–8 NABRE

With the speech of lips, and with another tongue he will
speak to this people. To whom he said: This is my rest, re-
fresh the weary, and this is my refreshing: and they would
not hear.

ISAIAS 28:11

On the seventh day God ended his work which he had
made: and he rested on the seventh day from all his work
which he had done. And he blessed the seventh day, and
sanctified it: because in it he had rested from all his work
which God created and made.

GENESIS 2:1–3

Yahweh says this, "Stand at the crossroads and look, ask for
the ancient paths: which was the good way? Take it and you
will find rest for yourselves."

JEREMIAH 6:16 NJB

Six days you shall do work: the seventh day shall be holy
unto you, the sabbath, and the rest of the Lord: he that shall
do any work on it.

EXODUS 35:2

I bless Yahweh who is my counselor, even at night my heart
instructs me. I keep Yahweh before me always, for with him
at my right hand, nothing can shake me. So my heart re-
joices, my soul delights, my body too will rest secure.

PSALM 16:7–9 NJB

Restoration

n.: The act of bringing someone or someone back to a former position or condition.

I will restore you to health; of your wounds I will heal you, says the Lord. "The outcast" they have called you, "with no avenger." Thus says the Lord: See!

JEREMIAH 30:17–18 NABRE

The threshing floors shall be full of grain, the vats shall overflow with wine and oil. I will restore to you the years which the swarming locust has eaten, the hopper, the destroyer, and the cutter, my great army, which I sent among you. You shall eat in plenty and be satisfied, and praise the name of the Lord your God, who has dealt wondrously with you. And my people shall never again be put to shame.

JOEL 2:24–26 RSV-CE

Now that I am old and gray, do not forsake me, God, That I may proclaim your might to all generations yet to come, Your power and justice, God, to the highest heaven. You have done great things; O God, who is your equal? You have sent me many bitter afflictions, but once more revive me. From the watery depths of the earth once more raise me up. Restore my honor; turn and comfort me, that I may praise you with the lyre for your faithfulness, my God, And sing to you with the harp, O Holy One of Israel! My lips will shout for joy as I sing your praise.

PSALM 71:18–23 NABRE

Stir up your power, come to save us. O Lord of hosts, restore us; Let your face shine upon us, that we may be saved.

PSALM 80:3–4 NABRE

Keep sober and alert, because your enemy the devil is on the prowl like a roaring lion, looking for someone to devour. Stand up to him, strong in faith and in the knowledge that it is the same kind of suffering that the community of your brothers throughout the world is undergoing. You will have to suffer only for a little while: the God of all grace who called you to eternal glory in Christ will restore you, he will confirm, strengthen and support you. His power lasts for ever and ever. Amen.

1 PETER 5:8–11 NJB

Create in me a clean heart, O God, and put a new and right spirit within me. Cast me not away from thy presence, and take not thy holy Spirit from me. Restore to me the joy of thy salvation, and uphold me with a willing spirit. Then I will teach transgressors thy ways, and sinners will return to thee.

PSALM 51:10–13 RSV-CE

You once favored, Lord, your land, restored the good fortune of Jacob. You forgave the guilt of your people, pardoned all their sins. Selah. You withdrew all your wrath, turned back your burning anger. Restore us once more, God our savior.

PSALM 85:2–5 NABRE

The Lord has done great things for us; we are glad. Restore our fortunes, O Lord, like the watercourses in the Negeb! May those who sow in tears reap with shouts of joy! He that goes forth weeping, bearing the seed for sowing, shall come home with shouts of joy, bringing his sheaves with him.

PSALM 126:3–6 RSV-CE

Lord of hosts, restore us; let your face shine upon us, that we may be saved.

PSALM 80:20 NABRE

Reverence

n.: A feeling of worshipful respect or honor.

Bid the older women likewise to be reverent in behavior, not to be slanderers or slaves to drink; they are to teach what is good, and so train the young women to love their husbands and children, to be sensible, chaste, domestic, kind, and submissive to their husbands, that the word of God may not be discredited.

Titus 2:3–5 RSV-CE

In your hearts reverence Christ as Lord. Always be prepared to make a defense to any one who calls you to account for the hope that is in you, yet do it with gentleness and reverence; and keep your conscience clear, so that, when you are abused, those who revile your good behavior in Christ may be put to shame.

1 Peter 3:15–16 RSV-CE

Let the whole earth fear Yahweh, let all who dwell in the world revere him; for, the moment he spoke, it was so, no sooner had he commanded, than there it stood! Yahweh thwarts the plans of nations, frustrates the counsels of peoples; but Yahweh's own plan stands firm for ever, his heart's counsel from age to age.

Psalm 33:8–11 NJB

He promiseth, saying: Yet once more, and I will move not only the earth, but heaven also. And in that he saith, Yet once more, he signifieth the translation of the moveable things as made, that those things may remain which are immoveable. Therefore receiving an immoveable kingdom, we have grace; whereby let us serve, pleasing God, with fear and reverence.

Hebrews 12:26–28

Come, let us bow low and do reverence; kneel before Yahweh who made us! For he is our God, and we the people of his sheepfold, the flock of his hand. If only you would listen to him today!

PSALM 95:6–7 NJB

O Lord, may your ear be attentive to my prayer and that of all your willing servants who revere your name.

NEHEMIAH 1:11 NABRE

The Law of Yahweh is perfect, refreshment to the soul; the decree of Yahweh is trustworthy, wisdom for the simple. The precepts of Yahweh are honest, joy for the heart; the commandment of Yahweh is pure, light for the eyes. The [reverential] fear of Yahweh is pure, lasting for ever; the judgments of Yahweh are true, upright, every one, more desirable than gold, even than the finest gold; his words are sweeter than honey, that drips from the comb.

PSALM 19:7–10 NJB

Come, my children, listen to me, I will teach you the [reverential] fear of Yahweh. Who among you delights in life, longs for time to enjoy prosperity? Guard your tongue from evil, your lips from any breath of deceit. Turn away from evil and do good, seek peace and pursue it. The eyes of Yahweh are on the upright, his ear turned to their cry.

PSALM 34:11–15 NJB

My child, if you take my words to heart, if you set store by my commandments, tuning your ear to wisdom, tuning your heart to understanding, yes, if your plea is for clear perception, if you cry out for understanding, if you look for it as though for silver, search for it as though for buried treasure, then you will understand what the [reverential] fear of Yahweh is, and discover the knowledge of God.

PROVERBS 2:1–5 NJB

Reward

n.: Something given or offered in return for a service.

I, the Lord, alone probe the mind and test the heart, To reward everyone according to his ways, according to the merit of his deeds.

JEREMIAH 17:10 NABRE

Whatever your task, work heartily, as serving the Lord and not men, knowing that from the Lord you will receive the inheritance as your reward; you are serving the Lord Christ.

COLOSSIANS 3:23–24 RSV-CE

Neither he that planteth is any thing, nor he that watereth; but God that giveth the increase. Now he that planteth, and he that watereth, are one. And every man shall receive his own reward, according to his own labour.

1 CORINTHIANS 3:6–8

Behold, I come quickly; and my reward is with me, to render to every man according to his works. I am Alpha and Omega, the first and the last, the beginning and the end.

REVELATION 22:12–13

By faith Moses, when he was grown up, denied himself to be the son of Pharao's daughter; rather choosing to be afflicted with the people of God, than to have the pleasure of sin for a time, esteeming the reproach of Christ greater riches than the treasure of the Egyptians. For he looked unto the reward.

HEBREWS 11:24–26

Without faith it is impossible to please God. For he that cometh to God, must believe that he is, and is a rewarder to them that seek him.

HEBREWS 11:6

Every man's work shall be manifest; for the day of the Lord shall declare it, because it shall be revealed in fire; and the fire shall try every man's work, of what sort it is. If any man's work abide, which he hath built thereupon, he shall receive a reward.

1 Corinthians 3:13–14

This is the commandment, that, as you have heard from the beginning, you should walk in the same: For many seducers are gone out into the world, who confess not that Jesus Christ is come in the flesh: this is a seducer and an antichrist. Look to yourselves, that you lose not the things which you have wrought: but that you may receive a full reward.

2 John 1:6–8

Love ye your enemies: do good, and lend, hoping for nothing thereby: and your reward shall be great, and you shall be the sons of the Highest; for he is kind to the unthankful, and to the evil.

Luke 6:35

Blessed are ye when they shall revile you, and persecute you, and speak all that is evil against you, untruly, for my sake: be glad and rejoice, for your reward is very great in heaven.

Matthew 5:11–12

He that receiveth a prophet in the name of a prophet, shall receive the reward of a prophet: and he that receiveth a just man in the name of a just man, shall receive the reward of a just man. And whosoever shall give to drink to one of these little ones a cup of cold water only in the name of a disciple, amen I say to you, he shall not lose his reward.

Matthew 10:41–32

Riches & Possessions

n.: Things that you own or have
with you at any given time.

Lay not up to yourselves treasures on earth: where the rust, and moth consume, and where thieves break through, and steal. But lay up to yourselves treasures in heaven: where neither the rust nor moth doth consume, and where thieves do not break through, nor steal. For where thy treasure is, there is thy heart also.

MATTHEW 6:19–21

Tell the rich in the present age not to be proud and not to rely on so uncertain a thing as wealth but rather on God, who richly provides us with all things for our enjoyment. Tell them to do good, to be rich in good works, to be generous, ready to share, thus accumulating as treasure a good foundation for the future, so as to win the life that is true life.

1 TIMOTHY 6:17–19 NABRE

My dearest brethren: Hath not God chosen the poor in this world, rich in faith and heirs of the kingdom which God hath promised to them that love him?

JAMES 2:5

Let the brother of low condition glory in his exaltation: And the rich, in his being low: because as the flower of the grass shall he pass away. For the sun rose with a burning heat and parched the grass: and the flower thereof fell off, and the beauty of the shape thereof perished. So also shall the rich man fade away in his ways.

JAMES 1:9–11

Labour not to be rich: but set bounds to thy prudence. Lift not up thy eyes to riches which thou canst not have: because they shall make themselves wings like those of an eagle, and shall fly towards heaven.

Proverbs 23:4–5

Hallelujah! Happy are those who fear the Lord, who greatly delight in God's commands. Their descendants shall be mighty in the land, generation upright and blessed. Wealth and riches shall be in their homes; their prosperity shall endure forever.

Psalm 112:1–3 nabre

God (who is rich in mercy) for his exceeding charity where-with he loved us. Even when we were dead in sins, hath quickened us together in Christ (by whose grace you are saved) and hath raised us up together and hath made us sit together in the heavenly places, through Christ Jesus. That he might shew in the ages to come the abundant riches of his grace, in his bounty towards us in Christ Jesus.

Ephesians 2:4–7

I will say to my soul: "My soul, you have plenty of good things laid by for many years to come; take things easy, eat, drink, have a good time." But God said to him, "Fool! This very night the demand will be made for your soul; and this hoard of yours, whose will it be then?" So it is when some-one stores up treasure for himself instead of becoming rich in the sight of God.

Luke 12:10–21 njb

Better someone poor living an honest life than someone of devious ways however rich.

Proverbs 28:6 njb

Righteousness

n.: The process and result of acting rightly;
the state of doing the right thing.

No human being will be justified in his sight by works of the
law, since through the law comes knowledge of sin. But now
the righteousness of God has been manifested apart from
law, although the law and the prophets bear witness to it, the
righteousness of God through faith in Jesus Christ for all
who believe.

ROMANS 3:20–22 RSV-CE

Yield yourselves to God as men who have been brought
from death to life, and your members to God as instru-
ments of righteousness. Do you not know that if you yield
yourselves to any one as obedient slaves, you are slaves of the
one whom you obey, either of sin, which leads to death, or of
obedience, which leads to righteousness? But thanks be to
God, that you who were once slaves of sin have become obedient from the heart to the standard of teaching to which
you were committed, and, having been set free from sin,
have become slaves of righteousness.

ROMANS 6:13, 16–18 RSV-CE

This is my prayer: that your love may increase ever more and
more in knowledge and every kind of perception, to discern
what is of value, so that you may be pure and blameless for
the day of Christ, filled with the fruit of righteousness that
comes through Jesus Christ for the glory and praise of God.

PHILIPPIANS 1:9–11 NABRE

Justice will dwell in the wilderness, and righteousness abide in
the fruitful field. And the effect of righteousness will be peace,
and the result of righteousness, quietness and trust for ever.

ISAIAH 32:16–17 RSV-CE

Sow for yourselves righteousness, reap the fruit of steadfast love; break up your fallow ground, for it is the time to seek the Lord, that he may come and rain salvation upon you.

HOSEA 10:12 RSV-CE

Blessed are they who hunger and thirst for righteousness, for they will be satisfied.

MATTHEW 5:6 NABRE

We are ambassadors for Christ, God making his appeal through us. We beseech you on behalf of Christ, be reconciled to God. For our sake he made him to be sin who knew no sin, so that in him we might become the righteousness of God.

2 CORINTHIANS 5:20–21 RSV-CE

He [Jesus] committed no sin, and no deceit was found in his mouth. When he was insulted, he returned no insult; when he suffered, he did not threaten; instead, he handed himself over to the one who judges justly. He himself bore our sins in his body upon the cross, so that, free from sin, we might live for righteousness.

1 PETER 2:22–24 NABRE

If any one purifies himself from what is ignoble, then he will be a vessel for noble use, consecrated and useful to the master of the house, ready for any good work. So shun youthful passions and aim at righteousness, faith, love, and peace, along with those who call upon the Lord from a pure heart.

2 TIMOTHY 2:21–22 RSV-CE

The wisdom from above is first pure, then peaceable, gentle, open to reason, full of mercy and good fruits, without uncertainty or insincerity. And the harvest of righteousness is sown in peace by those who make peace.

JAMES 3:17–18 RSV-CE

Sacrifice

n.: A giving up of something for
the sake of something else.

God is present as my helper; the Lord sustains my life. Turn back the evil upon my foes; in your faithfulness, destroy them. Then I will offer you generous sacrifice and praise your gracious name, Lord, because it has rescued me from every trouble.

PSALM 54:6–9 NABRE

Lord, open my lips; my mouth will proclaim your praise. For you do not desire sacrifice; a burnt offering you would not accept. My sacrifice, God, is a broken spirit; God, do not spurn a broken, humbled heart.

PSALM 51:17–19 NABRE

By him therefore let us offer the sacrifice of praise always to God, that is to say, the fruit of lips confessing to his name. And do not forget to do good, and to impart; for by such sacrifices God's favor is obtained.

HEBREWS 13:15–16

He [Jesus] is able for all time to save those who draw near to God through him, since he always lives to make intercession for them. For it was fitting that we should have such a high priest, holy, blameless, unstained, separated from sinners, exalted above the heavens. He has no need, like those high priests, to offer sacrifices daily, first for his own sins and then for those of the people; he did this once for all when he offered up himself. Indeed, the law appoints men in their weakness as high priests, but the word of the oath, which came later than the law, appoints a Son who has been made perfect for ever.

HEBREWS 7:25–28 RSV-CE

Coming, as to a living stone, rejected indeed by men, but chosen and made honourable by God: Be you also as living stones built up, a spiritual house, a holy priesthood, to offer up spiritual sacrifices, acceptable to God by Jesus Christ.

1 Peter 2:4–5

I beseech you therefore, brethren, by the mercy of God, that you present your bodies a living sacrifice, holy, pleasing unto God, your reasonable service. And be not conformed to this world; but be reformed in the newness of your mind, that you may prove what is the good, and the acceptable, and the perfect will of God.

Romans 12:1–2

Every one that hath left house, or brethren, or sisters, or father, or mother, or wife, or children, or lands for my name's sake, shall receive an hundredfold, and shall possess life everlasting.

Matthew 19:29

Is Yahweh pleased by burnt offerings and sacrifices or by obedience to Yahweh's voice? Truly, obedience is better than sacrifice.

1 Samuel 15:22 njb

The scribe said to him, "Well said, teacher. You are right in saying, 'He is One and there is no other than he.' And 'to love him with all your heart, with all your understanding, with all your strength, and to love your neighbor as yourself' is worth more than all burnt offerings and sacrifices."

Mark 12:32–33 nabre

Walk in love, as Christ also hath loved us, and hath delivered himself for us, an oblation and a sacrifice to God for an odor of sweetness.

Ephesians 5:2

Salvation

*n.: The condition of being free from
sin and its penalties and preserved
from destruction or failure.*

Knowing the season; that it is now the hour for us to rise
from sleep. For now our salvation is nearer than when we
believed. The night is passed, and the day is at hand. Let us
therefore cast off the works of darkness, and put on the armor of light. Let us walk honestly, as in the day: not in riot-
ing and drunkenness, not in chambering and impurities, not
in contention and envy: But put ye on the Lord Jesus Christ,
and make not provision for the flesh in its concupiscences.

ROMANS 13:11–14

If the word, spoken by angels, became steadfast, and every
transgression and disobedience received a just recompense
of reward: How shall we escape if we neglect so great salvation? which having begun to be declared by the Lord, was
confirmed unto us by them that heard him. God also bearing them witness by signs, and wonders, and divers miracles,
and distributions of the Holy Ghost, according to his own
will. For God hath not subjected unto angels the world to
come, whereof we speak.

HEBREWS 2:2–5

Let us, who are of the day, be sober, having on the breastplate of faith and charity, and for a helmet the hope of salvation. For God hath not appointed us unto wrath, but unto
the purchasing of salvation by our Lord Jesus Christ, Who
died for us; that, whether we watch or sleep, we may live together with him. For which cause comfort one another; and
edify one another, as you also do.

1 THESSALONIANS 5:8–11

My dearly beloved, (as you have always obeyed, not as in my presence only, but much more now in my absence,) with fear and trembling work out your salvation. For it is God who worketh in you, both to will and to accomplish, according to his good will. And do ye all things without murmurings and hesitations; That you may be blameless, and sincere children of God, without reproof, in the midst of a crooked and perverse generation; among whom you shine as lights in the world.

PHILIPPIANS 2:12–15

Laying away all malice, and all guile, and dissimulations, and envies, and all detractions, As newborn babes, desire the rational milk without guile, that thereby you may grow unto salvation: If so be you have tasted that the Lord is sweet.

1 PETER 2:1–3

Receive not the grace of God in vain. For he saith: In an accepted time have I heard thee; and in the day of salvation have I helped thee. Behold, now is the acceptable time; behold, now is the day of salvation.

2 CORINTHIANS 6:1–2

The Lord is my strength and my praise, and he is become salvation to me: he is my God and I will glorify him: the God of my father, and I will exalt him.

EXODUS 15:2

For God alone my soul waits in silence; from him comes my salvation. He only is my rock and my salvation, my fortress; I shall not be greatly moved.

PSALM 62:1–2 RSV-CE

Being consummated, he [Jesus] became, to all that obey him, the cause of eternal salvation.

HEBREWS 5:9

Scripture
*n.: The entirety of the Bible or a particular
passage from the Bible.*

From thy infancy thou hast known the holy scriptures which
can instruct thee to salvation by the faith which is in Christ
Jesus. All scripture, inspired of God, is profitable to teach,
to reprove, to correct, to instruct in justice: That the man of
God may be perfect, furnished to every good work.

2 TIMOTHY 3:15–17

The word of God is living and effectual and more piercing
than any two edged sword; and reaching unto the division
of the soul and the spirit, of the joints also and the marrow:
and is a discerner of the thoughts and intents of the heart.

HEBREWS 4:12

What things soever were written, were written for our learning: that through patience and the comfort of the scriptures,
we might have hope.

ROMANS 15:4

He [Jesus] said to them: These are the words which I spoke
to you, while I was yet with you, that all things must needs
be fulfilled, which are written in the law of Moses, and in
the prophets, and in the psalms, concerning me. Then he
opened their understanding, that they might understand
the scriptures. And he said to them: Thus it is written, and
thus it behoved Christ to suffer, and to rise again from the
dead, the third day: And that penance and remission of sins
should be preached in his name, unto all nations, beginning
at Jerusalem.

LUKE 24:44–47

Humbly welcome the Word which has been planted in you and can save your souls. But you must do what the Word tells you and not just listen to it and deceive yourselves. Anyone who listens to the Word and takes no action is like someone who looks at his own features in a mirror and, once he has seen what he looks like, goes off and immediately forgets it. But anyone who looks steadily at the perfect law of freedom and keeps to it—not listening and forgetting, but putting it into practice—will be blessed in every undertaking.

JAMES 1:21–25 NJB

The scripture hath concluded all under sin, that the promise, by the faith of Jesus Christ, might be given to them that believe.

GALATIANS 3:22

Being born again not of corruptible seed, but incorruptible, by the word of God who liveth and remaineth for ever. For all flesh is as grass; and all the glory thereof as the flower of grass. The grass is withered, and the flower thereof is fallen away. But the word of the Lord endureth for ever. And this is the word which by the gospel hath been preached unto you.

1 PETER 1:23–25

The Revelation of Jesus Christ, which God gave unto him, to make known to his servants the things which must shortly come to pass: and signified, sending by his angel to his servant John, Who hath given testimony to the word of God, and the testimony of Jesus Christ, what things soever he hath seen. Blessed is he, that readeth and heareth the words of this prophecy; and keepeth those things which are written in it; for the time is at hand.

REVELATION 1:1–3

Seeking God

v.: To actively pursue relationship with God;
to strive to know Him on a personal level.

When you call me, when you go to pray to me, I will listen to you. When you look for me, you will find me. Yes, when you seek me with all your heart, you will find me with you, says the Lord.

JEREMIAH 29:12–14 NABRE

"Come," says my heart, "seek God's face"; your face, Lord, do I seek! Do not hide your face from me; do not repel your servant in anger. You are my help; do not cast me off; do not forsake me, God my savior! Even if my father and mother forsake me, the Lord will take me in.

PSALM 27:8–10 NABRE

How can a young man keep his way spotless? By keeping your words. With all my heart I seek you, do not let me stray from your commandments.

PSALM 119:9–10 NJB

Seek ye the Lord, while he may be found: call upon him, while he is near. Let the wicked forsake his way, and the unjust man his thoughts, and let him return to the Lord, and he will have mercy on him, and to our God: for he is bountiful to forgive.

ISAIAS 55:6–7

Know the God of thy father, and serve him with a perfect heart, and a willing mind: for the Lord searcheth all hearts, and understandeth all the thoughts of minds. If thou seek him, thou shalt find him.

1 CHRONICLES 28:9

Alleluia! Give thanks to Yahweh, call on his name, proclaim his deeds to the peoples! Sing to him, make music for
him, recount all his wonders! Glory in his holy name, let
the hearts that seek Yahweh rejoice! Seek Yahweh and his
strength, tirelessly seek his presence!

Psalm 105:1–4

Without faith it is impossible to please God. For he that
cometh to God, must believe that he is, and is a rewarder to
them that seek him.

Hebrews 11:6

Let the hearts of those who seek the Lord rejoice! Seek
the Lord and his strength, seek his presence continually!
Remember the wonderful works that he has done, the
wonders he wrought, the judgments he uttered.

1 Chronicles 16:10–12 rsv-ce

When thou shalt seek there the Lord thy God, thou shalt
find him: yet so, if thou seek him with all thy heart, and all
the affliction of thy soul.

Deuteronomy 4:29

The clean of hand and pure of heart, who are not devoted to
idols, who have not sworn falsely. They will receive blessings
from the Lord, and justice from their saving God. Such are
the people that love the Lord, that seek the face of the God
of Jacob. Selah.

Psalm 24:4–6 nabre

My people, upon whom my name is called, being converted,
shall make supplication to me, and seek out my face, and do
penance for their most wicked ways: then will I hear from
heaven, and will forgive their sins and will heal their land.

2 Chronicles 7:14

Self-Control

n.: The ability to control your own actions, thoughts, and speech.

The end of all things is near, so keep your minds calm and sober for prayer. Above all preserve an intense love for each other, since love covers over many a sin.

1 Peter 4:7–8 njb

Therefore, let us not sleep as the rest do, but let us stay alert and sober. Those who sleep go to sleep at night, and those who are drunk get drunk at night. But since we are of the day, let us be sober, putting on the breastplate of faith and love and the helmet that is hope for salvation.

1 Thessalonians 5:6–8 nabre

The fruit of the Spirit is love, joy, peace, patience, kindness, generosity, faithfulness, gentleness, self-control. Against such there is no law. Now those who belong to Christ (Jesus) have crucified their flesh with its passions and desires. If we live in the Spirit, let us also follow the Spirit.

Galatians 5:22–25 nabre

Let no temptation take hold on you, but such as is human. And God is faithful, who will not suffer you to be tempted above that which you are able: but will make also with temptation issue, that you may be able to bear it.

1 Corinthians 10:12–13

Gird up your minds, be sober, set your hope fully upon the grace that is coming to you at the revelation of Jesus Christ. As obedient children, do not be conformed to the passions of your former ignorance, but as he who called you is holy, be holy yourselves in all your conduct; since it is written, "You shall be holy, for I am holy."

1 Peter 1:13–16 rsv-ce

Watch ye, and pray that ye enter not into temptation. The spirit indeed is willing, but the flesh weak.

MATTHEW 26:41

His divine power has bestowed on us everything that makes for life and devotion, through the knowledge of him who called us by his own glory and power. Through these, he has bestowed on us the precious and very great promises, so that through them you may come to share in the divine nature, after escaping from the corruption that is in the world because of evil desire. For this very reason, make every effort to supplement your faith with virtue, virtue with knowledge, knowledge with self-control, self-control with endurance, endurance with devotion, devotion with mutual affection, mutual affection with love. If these are yours and increase in abundance, they will keep you from being idle or unfruitful in the knowledge of our Lord Jesus Christ.

2 PETER 1:3–8 NABRE

You must say what is consistent with sound doctrine, namely, that older men should be temperate, dignified, self-controlled, sound in faith, love, and endurance. Similarly, older women should be reverent in their behavior, not slanderers, not addicted to drink, teaching what is good, so that they may train younger women to love their husbands and children, to be self-controlled, chaste, good homemakers, under the control of their husbands, so that the word of God may not be discredited. Urge the younger men, similarly, to control themselves, showing yourself as a model of good deeds in every respect, with integrity in your teaching, dignity, and sound speech that cannot be criticized, so that the opponent will be put to shame without anything bad to say about you.

TITUS 2:1–8 NABRE

Servanthood

n.: The ability to submit to others for the
purpose of good and sacrificial service.

What doth the Lord thy God require of thee, but that thou fear the Lord thy God, and walk in his ways, and love him, and serve the Lord thy God, with all thy heart, and with all thy soul: And keep the commandments of the Lord, and his ceremonies, which I command thee this day, that it may be well with thee?

DEUTERONOMY 10:12–13

After he [Jesus] had washed their feet, and taken his garments, being set down again, he said to them: Know you what I have done to you? You call me Master, and Lord; and you say well, for so I am. If then I being your Lord and Master, have washed your feet; you also ought to wash one another's feet. For I have given you an example, that as I have done to you, so you do also. Amen, amen I say to you: The servant is not greater than his lord; neither is the apostle greater than he that sent him.

JOHN 13:12–16

You are my friends, if you do the things that I command you. I will not now call you servants: for the servant knoweth not what his lord doth. But I have called you friends: because all things whatsoever I have heard of my Father, I have made known to you.

JOHN 15:14–15

Follow the Lord your God, and fear him, and keep his commandments, and hear his voice: him you shall serve, and to him you shall cleave.

DEUTERONOMY 13:4

Let the greatest among you be as the youngest, and the leader as the servant. For who is greater: the one seated at table or the one who serves? Is it not the one seated at table? I am among you as the one who serves. It is you who have stood by me in my trials; and I confer a kingdom on you, just as my Father has conferred one on me, that you may eat and drink at my table in my kingdom.

LUKE 22:26–30 NABRE

Whoever preaches, let it be with the words of God; whoever serves, let it be with the strength that God supplies, so that in all things God may be glorified through Jesus Christ, to whom belong glory and dominion forever and ever. Amen.

I PETER 4:11 NABRE

Let this mind be in you, which was also in Christ Jesus: who being in the form of God, thought it not robbery to be equal with God: but emptied himself, taking the form of a servant, being made in the likeness of men, and in habit found as a man. He humbled himself, becoming obedient unto death, even to the death of the cross. For which cause God also hath exalted him, and hath given him a name which is above all names: that in the name of Jesus every knee should bow, of those that are in heaven, on earth, and under the earth.

PHILIPPIANS 2:5–10

Whoever wishes to be great among you will be your servant; whoever wishes to be first among you will be the slave of all. For the Son of Man did not come to be served but to serve and to give his life as a ransom for many.

MARK 10:43–45 NABRE

Sin

*n.: An offense against moral law as
defined by a holy and just God.*

Thou, our God, art gracious and true, patient, and ordering
all things in mercy. For if we sin, we are thine, knowing thy
greatness: and if we sin not, we know that we are counted
with thee. For to know thee is perfect justice: and to know
thy justice, and thy power, is the root of immortality.

WISDOM 15:1–3

If we say, "We have no sin," we are deceiving ourselves, and
truth has no place in us; if we acknowledge our sins, he is
trustworthy and upright, so that he will forgive our sins and
will cleanse us from all evil.

1 JOHN 1:8–9 NJB

Let not sin therefore reign in your mortal body, so as to obey
the lusts thereof. Neither yield ye your members as instru-
ments of iniquity unto sin: but present yourselves to God, as
those that are alive from the dead; and your members as in-
struments of justice unto God. For sin shall not have dominion over you: for you are not under the law, but under grace.

ROMANS 6:12–14

My little children, these things I write to you, that you may
not sin. But if any man sin, we have an advocate with the
Father, Jesus Christ the just. And he is the propitiation
for our sins: and not for ours only, but also for those of the
whole world.

1 JOHN 2:1–2

In my heart I treasure your promises, to avoid sinning
against you. Blessed are you, Yahweh, teach me your will!

PSALM 119:11–12 NJB

Brothers, even if a person is caught in some transgression, you who are spiritual should correct that one in a gentle spirit, looking to yourself, so that you also may not be tempted. Bear one another's burdens, and so you will fulfill the law of Christ.

GALATIANS 6:1–2 NABRE

Looking on Jesus, the author and finisher of faith, who, having joy set before him, endured the cross, despising the shame, and now sitteth on the right hand of the throne of God. For think diligently upon him that endured such opposition from sinners against himself that you be not wearied, fainting in your minds. For you have not yet resisted unto blood, striving against sin.

HEBREWS 12:2–4

John saw Jesus coming to him; and he saith: Behold the Lamb of God. Behold him who taketh away the sin of the world.

JOHN 1:29

If thy brother sin against thee, reprove him: and if he do penance, forgive him. And if he sin against thee seven times in a day, and seven times in a day be converted unto thee, saying: I repent: forgive him.

LUKE 17:3–4

Happy the sinner whose fault is removed, whose sin is forgiven. Happy those to whom the Lord imputes no guilt, in whose spirit is no deceit.

PSALM 32:1–2 NABRE

Spiritual Thirst

*n.: A deep, compelling longing to understand spiritual
matters and know God in a personal way.*

As the deer longs for streams of water, so my soul longs
for you, O God. My being thirsts for God, the living God.
When can I go and see the face of God? My tears have been
my food day and night, as they ask daily, "Where is your
God?" Here deep calls to deep in the roar of your torrents.
All your waves and breakers sweep over me. At dawn may
the Lord bestow faithful love that I may sing praise through
the night, praise to the God of my life.

Psalm 42:2–5, 8 nabre

I stretch out my hands to thee; my soul thirsts for thee like
a parched land. [Selah] Make haste to answer me, O Lord!
My spirit fails! Hide not thy face from me, lest I be like
those who go down to the Pit. Let me hear in the morning
of thy steadfast love, for in thee I put my trust. Teach me the
way I should go, for to thee I lift up my soul.

Psalm 143:6–8

Some had lost their way in a barren desert; found no path
toward a city to live in. They were hungry and thirsty; their
life was ebbing away. In their distress they cried to the Lord
who rescued them in their peril, guided them by a direct
path so they reached a city to live in. Let them thank the
Lord for such kindness, such wondrous deeds for mere
mortals. For he satisfied the thirsty, filled the hungry with
good things.

Psalm 107:5–9 nabre

Blessed are they who hunger and thirst for righteousness, for they will be satisfied.

Matthew 5:6 nabre

O God, thou art my God, I seek thee, my soul thirsts for thee; my flesh faints for thee, as in a dry and weary land where no water is. So I have looked upon thee in the sanctuary, beholding thy power and glory. Because thy steadfast love is better than life, my lips will praise thee. So I will bless thee as long as I live; I will lift up my hands and call on thy name.

Psalm 63:1–4 rsv-ce

He that sat on the throne, said: Behold, I make all things new. And he said to me: Write, for these words are most faithful and true. And he said to me: It is done. I am Alpha and Omega; the beginning and the end. To him that thirsteth, I will give of the fountain of the water of life, freely.

Revelation 21:5–6

Thus saith the Lord: In an acceptable time I have heard thee, and in the day of salvation I have helped thee: and I have preserved thee, and given thee to be a covenant of the people, that thou mightest raise up the earth, and possess the inheritances that were destroyed: That thou mightest say to them that are bound: Come forth: and to them that are in darkness: shew yourselves. They shall feed in the ways, and their pastures shall be in every plain. They shall not hunger, nor thirst, neither shall the heat nor the sun strike them: for he that is merciful to them, shall be their shepherd, and at the fountains of waters he shall give them drink.

Isaias 49:8–10

Stewardship & Tithes

*n.: The careful and responsible management
of something entrusted to one's care.*

Each one of you has received a special grace, so, like good stewards responsible for all these varied graces of God, put it at the service of others. If anyone is a speaker, let it be as the words of God, if anyone serves, let it be as in strength granted by God; so that in everything God may receive the glory, through Jesus Christ, since to him alone belong all glory and power for ever and ever.

1 Peter 4:10–11 njb

Bring all the tithes into the storehouse, that there may be meat in my house, and try me in this, saith the Lord: if I open not unto you the flood-gates of heaven, and pour you out a blessing even to abundance. And I will rebuke for your sakes the devourer, and he shall not spoil the fruit of your land: neither shall the vine in the field be barren, saith the Lord of hosts. And all nations shall call you blessed: for you shall be a delightful land, saith the Lord of hosts.

Malachias 3:10–11

Honor the Lord with thy substance, and give him of the first of all thy fruits; And thy barns shall be filled with abundance, and thy presses shall run over with wine.

Proverbs 3:9–10

All goes well for those gracious in lending, who conduct their affairs with justice. They shall never be shaken; the just shall be remembered forever. They shall not fear an ill report; their hearts are steadfast, trusting the Lord.

Psalm 112:5–7 nabre

People should think of us as Christ's servants, stewards entrusted with the mysteries of God. In such a matter, what is expected of stewards is that each one should be found trustworthy.

1 CORINTHIANS 4:1–2 NJB

The Lord said: who (thinkest thou) is the faithful and wise steward, whom his lord setteth over his family, to give them their measure of wheat in due season? Blessed is that servant, whom when his lord shall come, he shall find so doing. Verily I say to you, he will set him over all that he possesseth.

LUKE 12:42–44

Before all things have a constant mutual charity among yourselves: for charity covereth a multitude of sins. Using hospitality one towards another, without murmuring, As every man hath received grace, ministering the same one to another: as good stewards of the manifold grace of God.

1 PETER 4:8–10

Well done, good and faithful servant, because thou hast been faithful over a few things, I will place thee over many things: enter thou into the joy of thy lord.

MATTHEW 25:21

Thou shalt set aside the tithes of all thy fruits that the earth bringeth forth, And thou shalt eat before the Lord thy God in the place which he shall choose, that his name may be called upon therein, the tithe of thy corn, and thy wine, and thy oil, and the firstborn of thy herds and thy sheep: that thou mayst learn to fear the Lord thy God at all times.

DEUTERONOMY 14:22–23

Strength

*n.: The state of being strong and
tough mentally or physically.*

He said to them, "Go your way, eat the fat and drink
sweet wine and send portions to him for whom nothing is
prepared; for this day is holy to our Lord; and do not be
grieved, for the joy of the Lord is your strength."

NEHEMIAH 8:10 RSV-CE

Yahweh is my strength and my shield, in him my heart
trusts. I have been helped; my body has recovered its vigor,
with all my heart I thank him. Yahweh is the strength of his
people, a safe refuge for his anointed.

PSALM 28:7–9 NJB

I will sing of thy might; I will sing aloud of thy steadfast
love in the morning. For thou hast been to me a fortress and
a refuge in the day of my distress. O my Strength, I will sing
praises to thee, for thou, O God, art my fortress, the God
who shows me steadfast love.

PSALM 59:16–17 RSV-CE

Therefore we also, from the day that we heard it, cease not to
pray for you and to beg that you may be filled with the knowledge of his will, in all wisdom and spiritual understanding:
That you may walk worthy of God, in all things pleasing; being fruitful in every good work and increasing in the knowledge of God: Strengthened with all might according to the
power of his glory, in all patience and longsuffering with joy.

COLOSSIANS 1:9–11

He gives strength to the weary, he strengthens the powerless. Youths grow tired and weary, the young stumble and fall, but those who hope in Yahweh will regain their strength, they will sprout wings like eagles, though they run they will not grow weary, though they walk they will never tire.

ISAIAH 40:29–31 NJB

Do not be afraid, for I am with you; do not be alarmed, for I am your God. I give you strength, truly I help you, truly I hold you firm with my saving right hand. Look, all those who rage against you will be put to shame and humiliated; those who picked quarrels with you will be reduced to nothing and will perish. You will look for them but will not find them, those who used to fight you; they will be destroyed and brought to nothing, those who made war on you. For I, Yahweh, your God, I grasp you by your right hand; I tell you, "Do not be afraid, I shall help you."

ISAIAH 41:10–13 NJB

Yours, O Lord, are grandeur and power, majesty, splendor, and glory. For all in heaven and on earth is yours; yours, O Lord, is the sovereignty; you are exalted as head over all. Riches and honor are from you, and you have dominion over all. In your hand are power and might; it is yours to give grandeur and strength to all. Therefore, our God, we give you thanks and we praise the majesty of your name. But who am I, and who are my people, that we should have the means to contribute so freely? For everything is from you, and we only give you what we have received from you.

1 CHRONICLES 29:11–14 NABRE

Suffering

n.: The state or experience of
feeling or enduring pain.

Whenever anyone bears the pain of unjust suffering because of consciousness of God, that is a grace. But what credit is there if you are patient when beaten for doing wrong? But if you are patient when you suffer for doing what is good, this is a grace before God. For to this you have been called, because Christ also suffered for you, leaving you an example that you should follow in his footsteps. "He committed no sin, and no deceit was found in his mouth." When he was insulted, he returned no insult; when he suffered, he did not threaten; instead, he handed himself over to the one who judges justly.

1 PETER 2:19–23 NABRE

In all things we suffer tribulation, but are not distressed; we are straitened, but are not destitute; We suffer persecution, but are not forsaken; we are cast down, but we perish not: Always bearing about in our body the mortification of Jesus, that the life also of Jesus may be made manifest in our bodies.

2 CORINTHIANS 4:8–10

I count all things to be but loss for the excellent knowledge of Jesus Christ, my Lord: for whom I have suffered the loss of all things and count them but as dung, that I may gain Christ. And may be found in him, not having my justice, which is of the law, but that which is of the faith of Christ Jesus, which is of God: justice in faith. That I may know him and the power of his resurrection and the fellowship of his sufferings: being made conformable to his death.

PHILIPPIANS 3:8–10

A faithful saying: for if we be dead with him, we shall live also with him. If we suffer, we shall also reign with him.

2 TIMOTHY 2:11–12

Remember thy word to thy servant, in which thou hast made me hope. This is my comfort in my affliction that thy promise gives me life. Godless men utterly deride me, but I do not turn away from thy law. When I think of thy ordinances from of old, I take comfort, O Lord.

PSALM 119:49–52 RSV-CE

The Spirit himself giveth testimony to our spirit that we are the sons of God. And if sons, heirs also; heirs indeed of God and joint heirs with Christ: yet so, if we suffer with him, that we may be also glorified with him. For I reckon that the sufferings of this time are not worthy to be compared with the glory to come that shall be revealed in us.

ROMANS 8:16–18

My dear friends, do not be taken aback at the testing by fire which is taking place among you, as though something strange were happening to you; but in so far as you share in the sufferings of Christ, be glad, so that you may enjoy a much greater gladness when his glory is revealed. If you are insulted for bearing Christ's name, blessed are you, for on you rests the Spirit of God, the Spirit of glory. None of you should ever deserve to suffer for being a murderer, a thief, a criminal or an informer; but if any one of you should suffer for being a Christian, then there must be no shame but thanksgiving to God for bearing this name.

1 PETER 4:12–16 NJB

Talents, Gifts & Skills

n.: The abilities, powers,
and gifts one is born with.

I remember your tears and long to see you again to complete
my joy. I also remember your sincere faith, a faith which first
dwelt in your grandmother Lois, and your mother Eunice,
and I am sure dwells also in you. That is why I am reminding
you now to fan into a flame the gift of God that you possess
through the laying on of my hands.

2 TIMOTHY 1:4–6 NJB

There are many different gifts, but it is always the same
Spirit; there are many different ways of serving, but it is always the same Lord. There are many different forms of activity, but in everybody it is the same God who is at work in
them all. The particular manifestation of the Spirit granted
to each one is to be used for the general good.

1 CORINTHIANS 12:4–7 NJB

To one is given from the Spirit the gift of utterance
expressing wisdom; to another the gift of utterance
expressing knowledge, in accordance with the same Spirit; to
another, faith, from the same Spirit; and to another, the gifts
of healing, through this one Spirit; to another, the working
of miracles; to another, prophecy; to another, the power of
distinguishing spirits; to one, the gift of different tongues
and to another, the interpretation of tongues. But at work in
all these is one and the same Spirit, distributing them at will
to each individual.

1 CORINTHIANS 12:8–11 NJB

The gifts and the calling of God are without repentance.

ROMANS 11:29

My dearest brethren. Every best gift, and every perfect gift, is from above, coming down from the Father of lights, with whom there is no change, nor shadow of alteration. For of his own will hath he begotten us by the word of truth, that we might be some beginning of his creatures.

JAMES 1:16–18

We being many, are one body in Christ, and every one members one of another. And having different gifts, according to the grace that is given us, either prophecy, to be used according to the rule of faith; Or ministry, in ministering; or he that teacheth, in doctrine; He that exhorteth, in exhorting; he that giveth, with simplicity; he that ruleth, with carefulness; he that sheweth mercy, with cheerfulness.

ROMANS 12:5–6

As every man hath received grace, ministering the same one to another: as good stewards of the manifold grace of God. If any man speak, let him speak, as the words of God. If any man minister, let him do it, as of the power, which God administereth: that in all things God may be honored through Jesus Christ: to whom is glory and empire for ever and ever. Amen.

1 PETER 4:10–11

Let no one have contempt for your youth, but set an example for those who believe, in speech, conduct, love, faith, and purity. Until I arrive, attend to the reading, exhortation, and teaching. Do not neglect the gift you have, which was conferred on you through the prophetic word.

1 TIMOTHY 4:12–14

I would that all men were even as myself: but every one hath his proper gift from God; one after this manner, and another after that.

1 CORINTHIANS 7:7

Temptation

n.: The state of being enticed to do wrong often
by the promise of pleasure or gain.

Blessed is the man who perseveres in temptation, for when
he has been proved he will receive the crown of life that
he promised to those who love him. No one experiencing
temptation should say, "I am being tempted by God"; for
God is not subject to temptation to evil, and he himself
tempts no one. Rather, each person is tempted when he is
lured and enticed by his own desire. Then desire conceives
and brings forth sin, and when sin reaches maturity it gives
birth to death.

JAMES 1:12–16 NJB

It behoved him in all things to be made like unto his brethren, that he might become a merciful and faithful high priest
before God, that he might be a propitiation for the sins of
the people. For in that wherein he himself hath suffered
and been tempted he is able to succor them also that are
tempted.

HEBREWS 2:17–18

Wherefore he that thinketh himself to stand, let him take
heed lest he fall. Let no temptation take hold on you, but
such as is human. And God is faithful, who will not suffer
you to be tempted above that which you are able: but will
make also with temptation issue, that you may be able to
bear it.

1 CORINTHIANS 10:12–13

Be subject therefore to God, but resist the devil, and he will fly
from you. Draw nigh to God, and he will draw nigh to you.

JAMES 4:7–8

Wherein he [Jesus] himself hath suffered and been tempted, he is able to succour them also that are tempted.

HEBREWS 2:18

Having therefore a great high priest that hath passed into the heavens, Jesus the Son of God: let us hold fast our confession. For we have not a high priest who cannot have compassion on our infirmities: but one tempted in all things like as we are, without sin. Let us go therefore with confidence to the throne of grace: that we may obtain mercy and find grace in seasonable aid.

HEBREWS 4:14–16

Put you on the armor of God, that you may be able to stand against the deceits of the devil. For our wrestling is not against flesh and blood; but against principalities and power, against the rulers of the world of this darkness, against the spirits of wickedness in the high places. Therefore take unto you the armor of God, that you may be able to resist in the evil day, and to stand in all things perfect. Stand therefore, having your loins girt about with truth, and having on the breastplate of justice, And your feet shod with the preparation of the gospel of peace: In all things taking the shield of faith, wherewith you may be able to extinguish all the fiery darts of the most wicked one. And take unto you the helmet of salvation, and the sword of the Spirit (which is the word of God).

EPHESIANS 6:11–17

I say then, walk in the spirit, and you shall not fulfill the lusts of the flesh. For the flesh lusteth against the spirit: and the spirit against the flesh; for these are contrary one to another: so that you do not the things that you would. But if you are led by the spirit, you are not under the law.

GALATIANS 5:16–18

Thankfulness

n.: Kindly or grateful thoughts;
expression of appreciation for the
consciousness of benefits received.

We ought to give thanks to God always for you, brethren, beloved of God, for that God hath chosen you firstfruits unto salvation, in sanctification of the spirit and faith of the truth: Whereunto also he hath called you by our gospel, unto the purchasing of the glory of our Lord Jesus Christ. Therefore, brethren, stand fast: and hold the traditions, which you have learned, whether by word or by our epistle.

2 THESSALONIANS 2:12–14

O give thanks to the Lord, for he is good; for his steadfast love endures for ever! Let them thank the Lord for his steadfast love, for his wonderful works to the sons of men! And let them offer sacrifices of thanksgiving, and tell of his deeds in songs of joy!

PSALM 107:1, 21–22 RSV-CE

Alleluia! I give thanks to Yahweh with all my heart, in the meeting-place of honest people, in the assembly. Great are the deeds of Yahweh, to be pondered by all who delight in them. Full of splendor and majesty his work, his saving justice stands firm for ever.

PSALM 111:1–3 NJB

Be ye filled with the holy Spirit, speaking to yourselves in psalms, and hymns, and spiritual canticles, singing and making melody in your hearts to the Lord; giving thanks always for all things, in the name of our Lord Jesus Christ, to God and the Father.

EPHESIANS 5:18–20

Giving thanks to God the Father, who hath made us worthy to be partakers of the lot of the saints in light: Who hath delivered us from the power of darkness and hath translated us into the kingdom of the Son of his love, in whom we have redemption through his blood, the remission of sins.

COLOSSIANS 1:12–14

I thank you, Lord, with all my heart; before the gods to you I sing. I bow low toward your holy temple; I praise your name for your fidelity and love. For you have exalted over all your name and your promise. When I cried out, you answered; you strengthened my spirit.

PSALM 138:1–3 NABRE

In all things give thanks for this is the will of God in Christ Jesus concerning you all.

1 THESSALONIANS 5:18

Thanks be to God, who always maketh us to triumph in Christ Jesus, and manifesteth the odor of his knowledge by us in every place. For we are the good odor of Christ unto God, in them that are saved, and in them that perish.

2 CORINTHIANS 2:14–15

Come, let us cry out with joy to Yahweh, acclaim the rock of our salvation. Let us come into his presence with thanksgiving, acclaim him with music. For Yahweh is a great God, a king greater than all the gods.

PSALM 95:1–3 NJB

O give thanks to the Lord, call on his name, make known his deeds among the peoples! Sing to him, sing praises to him, tell of all his wonderful works! Glory in his holy name.

1 CHRONICLES 16:8–10 RSV-CE

Thoughts

*n.: The result of mentally processing the images
and information captured by our minds.*

Never worry about anything; but tell God all your desires of
every kind in prayer and petition shot through with grati-
tude, and the peace of God which is beyond our understanding will guard your hearts and your thoughts in Christ Jesus.
Finally, brothers, let your minds be filled with everything
that is true, everything that is honorable, everything that is
upright and pure, everything that we love and admire—with
whatever is good and praiseworthy.

PHILIPPIANS 4:6–8 NJB

Let the wicked forsake his way, and the unjust man his
thoughts, and let him return to the Lord, and he will have
mercy on him, and to our God: for he is bountiful to forgive.
For my thoughts are not your thoughts: nor your ways my
ways, saith the Lord. For as the heavens are exalted above
the earth, so are my ways exalted above your ways, and my
thoughts above your thoughts.

ISAIAS 55:7–9

Who can detect heedless failings? Cleanse me from my
unknown faults. But from willful sins keep your servant; let
them never control me. Then shall I be blameless, innocent
of grave sin. Let the words of my mouth meet with your
favor, keep the thoughts of my heart before you, Lord, my
rock and my redeemer.

PSALM 19:13–15 NABRE

My son, attend to my wisdom, and incline thy ear to my prudence, that thou mayst keep thoughts, and thy lips may preserve instruction.

PROVERBS 5:1–2

He who teaches men knowledge, the Lord, knows the thoughts of man, that they are but a breath. Blessed is the man whom thou dost chasten, O Lord, and whom thou dost teach out of thy law.

PSALM 94:11–12 RSV-CE

O Lord, thou hast searched me and known me! Thou knowest when I sit down and when I rise up; thou discernest my thoughts from afar. Thou searchest out my path and my lying down, and art acquainted with all my ways. Even before a word is on my tongue, lo, O Lord, thou knowest it altogether.

PSALM 139:1–4 RSV-CE

I praise thee, for thou art fearful and wonderful. Wonderful are thy works! Thou knowest me right well; my frame was not hidden from thee, when I was being made in secret, intricately wrought in the depths of the earth. Thy eyes beheld my unformed substance; in thy book were written, every one of them, the days that were formed for me, when as yet there was none of them. How precious to me are thy thoughts, O God! How vast is the sum of them! If I would count them, they are more than the sand. When I awake, I am still with thee.

PSALM 139:14–18 RSV-CE

Trials

n.: Tests of faith, patience, or stamina.

The upright have Yahweh for their Saviour, their refuge in times of trouble; Yahweh helps them and rescues them, he will rescue them from the wicked, and save them because they take refuge in him.

PSALM 37:39–40 NJB

My brethren, count it all joy, when you shall fall into divers temptations: knowing that the trying of your faith worketh patience and patience hath a perfect work: that you may be perfect and entire, failing in nothing.

JAMES 1:2–4

Beloved, do not be surprised that a trial by fire is occurring among you, as if something strange were happening to you. But rejoice to the extent that you share in the sufferings of Christ, so that when his glory is revealed you may also rejoice exultantly. If you are insulted for the name of Christ, blessed are you, for the Spirit of glory and of God rests upon you.

1 PETER 4:12–14 NABRE

Be sober and watch: because your adversary the devil, as a roaring lion, goeth about seeking whom he may devour. Whom resist ye, strong in faith: knowing that the same affliction befalls your brethren who are in the world. But the God of all grace, who hath called us into his eternal glory in Christ Jesus, after you have suffered a little, will himself perfect you, and confirm you, and establish you.

1 PETER 5:8–10

We were approved by God that the gospel should be committed to us: even so we speak, not as pleasing men, but God, who proveth our hearts.

1 Thessalonians 2:4

Grant me justice, Lord! I have walked without blame. In the Lord I have trusted; I have not faltered. Test me, Lord, and try me; search my heart and mind.

Psalm 26:1–2 nabre

We faint not; but though our outward man is corrupted, yet the inward man is renewed day by day. For that which is at present momentary and light of our tribulation, worketh for us above measure exceedingly an eternal weight of glory. While we look not at the things which are seen, but at the things which are not seen. For the things which are seen, are temporal; but the things which are not seen, are eternal.

2 Corinthians 4:16–18

Though I live surrounded by trouble you give me life—to my enemies' fury! You stretch out your right hand and save me, Yahweh will do all things for me. Yahweh, your faithful love endures for ever, do not abandon what you have made.

Psalm 138:7–8 njb

The Lord knows how to rescue the devout from trial and to keep the unrighteous under punishment for the day of judgment.

2 Peter 2:9 nabre

When we were with you, we told you beforehand that we were to suffer affliction; just as it has come to pass, and as you know. For this reason, brethren, in all our distress and affliction we have been comforted about you through your faith; for now we live, if you stand fast in the Lord.

1 Thessalonians 3:4, 7–8 rsv-ce

Trust

n.: An assured reliance on the character, ability,
strength, or truth of someone or something.

Trust in the Lord and do good that you may dwell in the
land and live secure. Find your delight in the Lord who will
give you your heart's desire. Commit your way to the Lord;
trust that God will act and make your integrity shine like
the dawn, your vindication like noonday.

PSALM 37:3–7 NABRE

Blessed be the man that trusteth in the Lord, and the Lord
shall be his confidence. And he shall be as a tree that is
planted by the waters, that spreadeth out its roots towards
moisture: and it shall not fear when the heat cometh. And
the leaf thereof shall be green, and in the time of drought it
shall not be solicitous, neither shall it cease at any time to
bring forth fruit.

JEREMIAS 17:7–8

Blessed is the man who makes the Lord his trust, who does
not turn to the proud, to those who go astray after false
gods! Thou hast multiplied, O Lord my God, thy wondrous
deeds and thy thoughts toward us; none can compare with
thee! Were I to proclaim and tell of them, they would be
more than can be numbered.

PSALM 40:4–5 RSV-CE

Trust in the Lord with all your heart, on your own
intelligence rely not; In all your ways be mindful of him, and
he will make straight your paths.

PROVERBS 3:5–6 NABRE

Whoever trusts in Yahweh is like Mount Zion: unshakeable, it stands for ever. Jerusalem! The mountains encircle her: so Yahweh encircles his people, henceforth and for ever.

PSALM 125:1–2 NJB

Answer me quickly, Yahweh, my spirit is worn out; do not turn away your face from me, or I shall be like those who sink into oblivion. Let dawn bring news of your faithful love, for I place my trust in you; show me the road I must travel for you to relieve my heart.

PSALM 143:7–8 NJV

You who dwell in the shelter of the Most High, who abide in the shadow of the Almighty, say to the Lord, "My refuge and fortress, my God in whom I trust." God will rescue you from the fowler's snare, from the destroying plague, will shelter you with pinions, spread wings that you may take refuge; God's faithfulness is a protecting shield.

PSALM 91:1–4 NABRE

Many are the afflictions of the just; but out of them all will the Lord deliver them. The Lord keepeth all their bones, not one of them shall be broken. The death of the wicked is very evil: and they that hate the just shall be guilty. The Lord will redeem the souls of his servants: and none of them that trust in him shall offend.

PSALM 33:20–23

I trust in thee, O Lord, I say, "Thou art my God." My times are in thy hand; deliver me from the hand of my enemies and persecutors! Let thy face shine on thy servant; save me in thy steadfast love!

PSALM 31:14–16 RSV-CE

Truth

n.: The real and settled state of things; fact.

The God of patience and of comfort grant you to be of one mind one towards another, according to Jesus Christ: that with one mind, and with one mouth, you may glorify God and the Father of our Lord Jesus Christ.

ROMANS 15:5–6

He that walketh in justices, and speaketh truth, that casteth away avarice by oppression, and shaketh his hands from all bribes, that stoppeth his ears lest he hear blood, and shutteth his eyes that he may see no evil. He shall dwell on high, the fortifications of rocks shall be his highness: bread is given him, his waters are sure.

ISAIAS 33:15–16

Yahweh, who can find a home in your tent, who can dwell on your holy mountain? Whoever lives blamelessly, who acts uprightly, who speaks the truth from the heart.

PSALM 15:1–2 NJB

When he spoke these things, many believed in him. Then Jesus said to those Jews, who believed him: If you continue in my word, you shall be my disciples indeed. And you shall know the truth, and the truth shall make you free.

JOHN 8:30–32

Whither I go you know, and the way you know. Thomas saith to him: Lord, we know not whither thou goest; and how can we know the way? Jesus saith to him: I am the way, and the truth, and the life. No man cometh to the Father, but by me.

JOHN 14:4–6

I have yet many things to say to you: but you cannot bear them now. But when he, the Spirit of truth, is come, he will teach you all truth. For he shall not speak of himself; but what things soever he shall hear, he shall speak; and the things that are to come, he shall shew you.

JOHN 16:11–13

Jesus answered: My kingdom is not of this world. If my kingdom were of this world, my servants would certainly strive that I should not be delivered to the Jews: but now my kingdom is not from hence. Pilate therefore said to him: Art thou a king then? Jesus answered: Thou sayest that I am a king. For this was I born, and for this came I into the world; that I should give testimony to the truth. Every one that is of the truth, heareth my voice. Pilate saith to him: What is truth? And when he said this, he went out again to the Jews, and saith to them: I find no cause in him.

JOHN 18:36–38

We know that we are of God, and the whole world is seated in wickedness. And we know that the Son of God is come: and he hath given us understanding that we may know the true God, and may be in his true Son. This is the true God and life eternal.

JOHN 5:19–20

Behold, thou desirest truth in the inward being; therefore teach me wisdom in my secret heart. Purge me with hyssop, and I shall be clean; wash me, and I shall be whiter than snow.

PSALM 51:6–7 RSV-CE

Understanding

*n.: The result of grasping the meaning
of something; comprehension.*

I follow all your precepts; every wrong way I hate. Wonderful are your decrees; therefore I observe them. The revelation of your words sheds light, gives understanding to the simple.

PSALM 119:128–130 NABRE

Where is wisdom to be found, and where is the place of understanding? Man knoweth not the price thereof, neither is it found in the land of them that live in delights. The depth saith: It is not in me: and the sea saith: It is not with me. The finest gold shall not purchase it, neither shall silver be weighed in exchange for it.

JOB 28:11–15

Who among you is wise and understanding? Let him show his works by a good life in the humility that comes from wisdom.

JAMES 3:13 NABRE

We do not cease praying for you and asking that you may be filled with the knowledge of his will through all spiritual wisdom and understanding to live in a manner worthy of the Lord, so as to be fully pleasing, in every good work bearing fruit and growing in the knowledge of God, strengthened with every power, in accord with his glorious might, for all endurance and patience, with joy giving thanks to the Father, who has made you fit to share in the inheritance of the holy ones in light.

COLOSSIANS 1:9–12 NABRE

Get wisdom, get understanding! Do not forget or turn aside from the words I utter. Forsake her not, and she will preserve you; love her, and she will safeguard you; the beginning of wisdom is: get wisdom; at the cost of all you have, get understanding. Extol her, and she will exalt you; she will bring you honors if you embrace her; she will put on your head a graceful diadem; a glorious crown will she bestow on you.

PROVERBS 4:5–9 NABRE

I hoped that greater age would speak, and that a multitude of years would teach wisdom. But, as I see, there is a spirit in men, and the inspiration of the Almighty giveth understanding. They that are aged are not the wise men, neither do the ancients understand judgment.

JOB 32:7–9

I have more understanding than the aged because I keep your precepts. I restrain my foot from evil paths to keep your word. I do not turn aside from your judgments, because you yourself have instructed me. How pleasant your promise to my palate, sweeter than honey in my mouth!

PSALM 119:100–102 NJB

Whence then cometh wisdom? and where is the place of understanding? It is hid from the eyes of all living and the fowls of the air know it not. Destruction and death have said: With our ears we have heard the fame thereof. God understandeth the way of it, and he knoweth the place thereof. And he said to man: Behold the fear of the Lord, that is wisdom: and to depart from evil, is understanding.

JOB 28:20–23, 28

Unity

*n.: The condition or state of being one;
harmony; concord.*

Take every care to preserve the unity of the Spirit by the peace
that binds you together. There is one Body, one Spirit, just as
one hope is the goal of your calling by God. There is one Lord,
one faith, one baptism, and one God and Father of all, over all,
through all and within all. On each one of us God's favor has
been bestowed in whatever way Christ allotted it.

Ephesians 4:3–7 njb

Behold, how good and pleasant it is when brothers dwell
in unity! It is like the precious oil upon the head, running
down upon the beard, upon the beard of Aaron, running
down on the collar of his robes! It is like the dew of
Hermon, which falls on the mountains of Zion! For there
the Lord has commanded the blessing, life for evermore.

Psalm 133:1–3 rsv-ce

I beseech you, brethren, by the name of our Lord Jesus
Christ, that you all speak the same thing, and that there be
no schisms among you; but that you be perfect in the same
mind, and in the same judgment.

1 Corinthians 1:10

For as the body is one, and hath many members; and all the
members of the body, whereas they are many, yet are one
body, so also is Christ. For in one Spirit were we all baptized
into one body, whether Jews or Gentiles, whether bond or
free; and in one Spirit we have all been made to drink.

1 Corinthians 12:12–13

To some, his "gift" was that they should be apostles; to some prophets; to some, evangelists; to some, pastors and teachers; to knit God's holy people together for the work of service to build up the Body of Christ, until we all reach unity in faith and knowledge of the Son of God and form the perfect Man, fully mature with the fullness of Christ himself.

Ephesians 4:11–13 njb

The God of patience and of comfort grant you to be of one mind one towards another, according to Jesus Christ: that with one mind, and with one mouth, you may glorify God and the Father of our Lord Jesus Christ.

Romans 15:5–6

You should all agree among yourselves and be sympathetic; love the brothers, have compassion and be self-effacing. Never repay one wrong with another, or one abusive word with another; instead, repay with a blessing. That is what you are called to do, so that you inherit a blessing.

1 Peter 3:8–9 njb

Not for them only do I pray, but for them also who through their word shall believe in me; that they all may be one, as thou, Father, in me, and I in thee; that they also may be one in us; that the world may believe that thou hast sent me. And the glory which thou hast given me, I have given to them; that they may be one, as we also are one: I in them, and thou in me; that they may be made perfect in one: and the world may know that thou hast sent me, and hast loved them, as thou hast also loved me.

John 17:20–23

Victory

n.: The achievement of success in a struggle against odds or difficulties, enemies or opponents.

Today you are about to join battle with your enemies. Do not be faint hearted. Let there be no fear or trembling or alarm as you face them. Yahweh your God is marching with you, to fight your enemies for you and make you victorious.

DEUTERONOMY 20:3–4 NJB

The upright man pays heed to his ways. There is no wisdom, no understanding, no counsel, against the Lord. The horse is equipped for the day of battle, but victory is the Lord's.

PROVERBS 21:29–31 NABRE

Behold, I tell you a mystery. We shall all indeed rise again: but we shall not all be changed. In a moment, in the twinkling of an eye, at the last trumpet: for the trumpet shall sound, and the dead shall rise again incorruptible: and we shall be changed. For this corruptible must put on incorruption; and this mortal must put on immortality. And when this mortal hath put on immortality, then shall come to pass the saying that is written: Death is swallowed up in victory. O death, where is thy victory? O death, where is thy sting? Now the sting of death is sin: and the power of sin is the law. But thanks be to God, who hath given us the victory through our Lord Jesus Christ.

1 CORINTHIANS 15:51–57

We have thought on thy steadfast love, O God, in the midst of thy temple. As thy name, O God, so thy praise reaches to the ends of the earth. Thy right hand is filled with victory.

PSALM 48:9–10 RSV-CE

We will triumph with the help of God, who will trample down our foes.

PSALM 60:14 NABRE

Whosoever believeth that Jesus is the Christ, is born of God. And every one that loveth him who begot, loveth him also who is born of him. In this we know that we love the children of God: when we love God, and keep his commandments. For this is the charity of God, that we keep his commandments: and his commandments are not heavy. For whatsoever is born of God, overcometh the world: and this is the victory which overcometh the world, our faith. Who is he that overcometh the world, but he that believeth that Jesus is the Son of God?

1 JOHN 5:1–5

Who then shall separate us from the love of Christ? Shall tribulation? or distress? or famine? or nakedness? or danger? or persecution? or the sword? (As it is written: For thy sake we are put to death all the day long. We are accounted as sheep for the slaughter.) But in all these things we overcome, because of him that hath loved us.

ROMANS 8:35–37

These things I have spoken to you, that in me you may have peace. In the world you shall have distress: but have confidence, I have overcome the world.

JOHN 16:33

I come quickly: hold fast that which thou hast, that no man take thy crown. He that shall overcome, I will make him a pillar in the temple of my God.

REVELATION 3:11–12

Waiting

n.: A state or attitude of watchfulness and expectancy.

The way of the just is right, the path of the just is right to walk in. And in the way of thy judgments, O Lord, we have patiently waited for thee: thy name, and thy remembrance are the desire of the soul. My soul hath desired thee in the night: yea, and with my spirit within me in the morning early I will watch to thee.

Isaias 26:7–9

The Lord is my portion, said my soul: therefore will I wait for him. The Lord is good to them that hope in him, to the soul that seeketh him. It is good to wait with silence for the salvation of God.

Lamentations 3:24–26

Be still before the Lord; wait for God. Do not be provoked by the prosperous, nor by malicious schemers. Give up your anger, abandon your wrath; do not be provoked; it brings only harm. Those who do evil will be cut off, but those who wait for the Lord will possess the land. Wait a little, and the wicked will be no more; look for them and they will not be there.

Psalm 37:7–10 nabre

They shall say in that day: Lo, this is our God, we have waited for him, and he will save us: this is the Lord, we have patiently waited for him, we shall rejoice and be joyful in his salvation.

Isaias 25:9

With expectation I have waited for the Lord, and he was attentive to me. And he heard my prayers, and brought me out of the pit of misery and the mire of dregs. And he set my feet upon a rock, and directed my steps. And he put a new canticle into my mouth, a song to our God. Many shall see, and shall fear: and they shall hope in the Lord.

PSALM 40:2–4

I waited patiently for the Lord; he inclined to me and heard my cry. He drew me up from the desolate pit, out of the miry bog, and set my feet upon a rock, making my steps secure. He put a new song in my mouth, a song of praise to our God.

PSALM 40:1–3 RSV-CE

I wait for the Lord, my soul waits, and in his word I hope; my soul waits for the Lord more than watchmen for the morning, more than watchmen for the morning.

PSALM 130:5–6 RSV-CE

We look for new heavens and a new earth according to his promises, in which justice dwelleth. Wherefore, dearly beloved, waiting for these things, be diligent that you may be found before him unspotted and blameless in peace.

2 PETER 3:13–14

We are saved by hope. But hope that is seen, is not hope. For what a man seeth, why doth he hope for? But if we hope for that which we see not, we wait for it with patience.

ROMANS 8:24–25

Wisdom

*n.: The ability to discern inner qualities
and relationships; insight.*

Because the Lord giveth wisdom: and out of his mouth
cometh prudence and knowledge. He will keep the salvation
of the righteous, and protect them that walk in simplicity.
Keeping the paths of justice, and guarding the ways of
saints. Then shalt thou understand justice, and judgment,
and equity, and every good path. If wisdom shall enter into
thy heart, and knowledge please thy soul.

Proverbs 2:6–10

If at heart you have the bitterness of jealousy, or selfish ambition, do not be boastful or hide the truth with lies; this is
not the wisdom that comes from above, but earthly, human
and devilish. Wherever there are jealousy and ambition,
there are also disharmony and wickedness of every kind;
whereas the wisdom that comes down from above is essen-
tially something pure; it is also peaceable, kindly and consid-
erate; it is full of mercy and shows itself by doing good; nor
is there any trace of partiality or hypocrisy in it.

James 3:14–17 njb

Who is wise, and he shall understand these things? prudent,
and he shall know these things? For the ways of the Lord are
right, and the just shall walk in them: but the transgressors
shall fall in them.

Osee 14:10

God loveth none but him that dwelleth with wisdom. For
she is more beautiful than the sun, and above all the order of
the stars: being compared with the light, she is found before
it. For after this cometh night, but no evil can overcome
wisdom.

Wisdom 7:28–30

Wisdom is as good as a legacy, profitable to those who enjoy the light of the sun. For as money protects, so does wisdom, and the advantage of knowledge is this: that wisdom bestows life on those who possess her.

ECCLESIASTES 7:11–12 NJB

Rebuke a wise man, and he will love thee. Give an occasion to a wise man, and wisdom shall be added to him. The fear of the Lord is the beginning of wisdom: and the knowledge of the holy is prudence.

PROVERBS 9:8–10

Blessed is the man that findeth wisdom, and is rich in prudence: The purchasing thereof is better than the merchandise of silver, and her fruit than the chief and purest gold: She is more precious than all riches: and all the things that are desired, are not to be compared to her. Length of days is in her right hand, and in her left hand riches and glory. Her ways are beautiful ways, and all her paths are peaceable. She is a tree of life to them that lay hold on her: and he that shall retain her is blessed.

PROVERBS 3:13–18

I also, hearing of your faith that is in the Lord Jesus and of your love towards all the saints, Cease not to give thanks for you, making commemoration of you in my prayers, That the God of our Lord Jesus Christ, the Father of glory, may give unto you the spirit of wisdom and of revelation, in the knowledge of him.

EPHESIANS 1:15–17

Words

n.: Something that is said; talk or discourse.

If any man think himself to be religious, not bridling his tongue but deceiving his own heart, this man's religion is vain. Religion clean and undefiled before God and the Father is this: to visit the fatherless and widows in their tribulation and to keep one's self unspotted from this world.

JAMES 1:26–27

Hold the form of sound words which thou hast heard of me: in faith and in the love which is in Christ Jesus. Keep the good thing committed to thy trust by the Holy Ghost who dwelleth in us.

2 TIMOTHY 1:13–14

Exhort one another every day, whilst it is called to day, that none of you be hardened through the deceitfulness of sin. For we are made partakers of Christ: yet so, if we hold the beginning of his substance firm unto the end.

HEBREWS 3:13–14

A word fitly spoken is like apples of gold in a setting of silver. Like a gold ring or an ornament of gold is a wise reprover to a listening ear. Like the cold of snow in the time of harvest is a faithful messenger to those who send him, he refreshes the spirit of his masters.

PROVERBS 25:11–13 RSV-CE

An evil man is ensnared by the transgression of his lips, but the righteous escapes from trouble. From the fruit of his words a man is satisfied with good, and the work of a man's hand comes back to him.

PROVERBS 12:13–14 RSV-CE

Let your conversation be worthy of the gospel of Christ: that, whether I come and see you, or, being absent, may hear of you, that you stand fast in one spirit, with one mind labouring together for the faith of the gospel.

PHILIPPIANS 1:27

Let no evil speech proceed from your mouth: but that which is good, to the edification of faith: that it may administer grace to the hearers. And grieve not the holy Spirit of God: whereby you are sealed unto the day of redemption.

EPHESIANS 4:29–30

Out of the abundance of the heart the mouth speaketh. A good man out of a good treasure bringeth forth good things: and an evil man out of an evil treasure bringeth forth evil things.

MATTHEW 12:34–35

Conduct yourselves wisely toward outsiders, making the most of the time. Let your speech always be gracious, seasoned with salt, so that you may know how you ought to answer every one.

COLOSSIANS 4:5–6 RSV-CE

Let my prayer come before you; rescue me according to your promise. May my lips pour forth your praise, because you teach me your laws. May my tongue sing of your promise, for all your commands are just.

PSALM 119:170–172 NABRE

The mind of the wise man makes him eloquent, and augments the persuasiveness of his lips. Pleasing words are a honeycomb, sweet to the taste and healthful to the body.

PROVERBS 16:23–24 NABRE

Work

*n.: The use of strength or ability to
get something done.*

Each one must examine his own work, and then he will have
reason to boast with regard to himself alone, and not with
regard to someone else; for each will bear his own load.

GALATIANS 6:4–5 NABRE

Labour as a good soldier of Christ Jesus. No man, being a
soldier to God, entangleth himself with secular businesses:
that he may please him to whom he hath engaged himself.
For he also that striveth for the mastery is not crowned, except he strive lawfully. The husbandman that laboreth must
first partake of the fruits. Understand what I say: for the
Lord will give thee in all things understanding.

2 TIMOTHY 2:3–7

God is not unjust so as to overlook your work and the love
you have demonstrated for his name by having served and
continuing to serve the holy ones. We earnestly desire each
of you to demonstrate the same eagerness for the fulfillment
of hope until the end, so that you may not become sluggish,
but imitators of those who, through faith and patience, are
inheriting the promises.

HEBREWS 6:10–12 NABRE

Behold, what I have seen to be good and to be fitting is to
eat and drink and find enjoyment in all the toil with which
one toils under the sun the few days of his life which God
has given him, for this is his lot. Every man also to whom
God has given wealth and possessions and power to enjoy
them, and to accept his lot and find enjoyment in his toil—
this is the gift of God.

ECCLESIASTES 5:18–19 RSV-CE

My beloved brethren, be ye steadfast and unmoveable: always abounding in the work of the Lord, knowing that your labour is not in vain in the Lord.

1 Corinthians 15:58

Jesus answered: In all truth I tell you, you are looking for me not because you have seen the signs but because you had all the bread you wanted to eat. Do not work for food that goes bad, but work for food that endures for eternal life, which the Son of man will give you, for on him the Father, God himself, has set his seal.

John 6:26–27 njb

Work willingly for the sake of the Lord and not for the sake of human beings. Never forget that everyone, whether a slave or a free man, will be rewarded by the Lord for whatever work he has done well.

Ephesians 6:7–8 njb

I did the planting, Apollos did the watering, but God gave growth. In this, neither the planter nor the waterer counts for anything; only God, who gives growth. It is all one who does the planting and who does the watering, and each will have the proper pay for the work that he has done. After all, we do share in God's work; you are God's farm, God's building.

1 Corinthians 3:6–9 njb